Ghosts and Haunted Places of the American Civil War

Shannon Boyer Jones

With the Black Moon Paranormal Society

Copyright © 2012 Shannon Boyer Jones

All rights reserved.

ISBN:1480145068
ISBN-13:978-1480145061

OTHER BOOKS BY THE AUTHOR

GHOSTS AND HAUNTED PLACES OF PENNSYLVANIA

Shannon Boyer Jones

DEDICATION
MY FAMILY

Ghosts and Haunted Places of the American Civil War

CONTENTS

	Acknowledgments, Preface, The War, Top Ten Battles	I
1	Harpers Ferry	1
2	Andersonville and Rock Island Prisons	3
3	Antietam	9
4	Chickamauga	16
5	Chowan University	19
6	Corinth Battlefield	21
7	Creekside Inn	22
8	Franklin Battlefield, the Carnton Plantation and the Carter House	25
9	Fredericksburg	30
10	Fort McAllister	37
11	Fort Mifflin	39
12	Gettysburg	42
13	Iron Furnaces	64
14	Manassas	71
15	Shenandoah Valley	79
16	Point Lookout	82
	Glossary of Paranormal Terms	85
	Authors Note	

ACKNOWLEDGMENTS

I would like to thank all the members of the Black Moon Paranormal Society who helped with this book and shared their stories, evidence and photographs.

As well as: Danielle Mercilliott Steelman; Jennifer Bucher and Laura Fealtman for travelling with me.

Photographs are also courtesy of: Daniel Geyer and Morgan Gentry.

Through the actions of a war of brothers, we have forever marked an expanse of hallowed ground. The blood of men staining the land for eternity; For brotherly blood spilled in battle can never be wiped clean from a nation's history.

- Shannon Boyer Jones

Statue in honor of Sergeant Kirkland, Fredericksburg Battlefield

Preface

You walk along a lonely path in the night. Shadows dance in the darkness. Nocturnal creatures rustle in the bushes and up in the trees where tree frogs chirp and owls hoot until, for just a moment, all around becomes suddenly silent.

From within the darkness, a Snare drum taps from what sounds to be a distance and the muffled roar of gunfire echoes from a faraway place. A white mist blows before you and the air grows unusually, unnaturally cold. The mist before you shape shifts to that of an officer dressed in period clothing, his gray coat adorned with gold buttons and a belt, with high white cuffs, gray pants tucked into high boots and a saber at his side. He watches you for just a second, that seems to last for minutes. Then the sounds disappear and the apparition gently fades away from sight. Except not from memory...

THE WAR

As fast and loud as the first shots fired at Fort Sumter, South Carolina, the war between the states rang out through the nation. The fires of rebellion, abolition, freedom, justice and excitement spread like a fire in the forest; consuming everything in it's path.

"South Carolina will secede from the Union as surely as that night succeeds the day, and nothing can now prevent or delay it but a revolution at the North." -

South Carolinian William Trenholm in a letter to a friend.

The excitement is torn away by horror, the innocence of youth replaced by hardened wisdom and the war continued to go on.

"At last Lincoln threatens us with a proclamation abolishing slavery[1] - here in the free Southern Confederacy; and they say McClellan is deposed. They want more fighting -I mean the government, whose skins are safe, they want more fighting, and trust to luck for the skill of the new generals".

-Mary Boykin Miller Chesnut, 1823-1886, from her diary

Four long years passed from the first shots until the last; though it was brewing long before the official start of the war. During those four years, between 618,000 and 700,000 Americans died, more than the total of Americans from the Revolutionary War through to the Vietnam War.

"War loses a great deal of romance after a soldier has seen his first battle. I have a more vivid recollection of the first than the last one I was in. It is a classical maxim that it is sweet and

becoming to die for one's country; but whoever has seen the horrors of a battle-field feels that it is far sweeter to live for it." from Mosby's War Reminiscences by John S. Mosby

    All that is left of the war is the history, stories, artifacts, hallowed ground; and...apparitions, phantoms, ghosts and mysterious lights that glow in the night.

Top Ten Civil War Battles with the Highest Causalities

*Causalities: are defined as killed, wounded and missing in action.

1. Gettysburg , PA

Estimated Casualties 51,112

Union : 23,049 - 23,055

Confederate: 23,231 - 28,063

2. Chickamauga , VA

Estimated Casualties 34,624

Union : 16,170

Confederate: 18,454

3. Chancellorsville , VA

Estimated Casualties 30,099

Union : 17,278

Confederate: 12,821

4. Spotsylvania , VA

Estimated Casualties 27,399

Union : 18,399

Confederate: 9,000

5. Antietam , MD (the single bloodiest day)

Estimated Casualties 26,134

Union : 12,410

Confederate: 13,724

6. The Wilderness, VA

Estimated Casualties 25,416

Union : 17,666

Confederate: 7,750

7. Second Manassas , VA

Estimated Casualties 25,251

Union : 16,054

Confederate: 9,197

8. Stone's River, TN

Estimated Casualties 24,645

Union : 12,906

Confederate: 11,739

9. Shiloh , TN

Estimated Casualties 23,741

Union : 13,047

Confederate: 10,694

10. Fort Donelson , TN

Estimated Casualties 19,455

Union : 2,832

Confederate: 16,623

HARPERS FERRY
WEST VIRGINIA

Maryland Heights, overlooking Harpers Ferry

Quaint, cozy buildings line the streets; reminiscent, more-so, of over a century past instead of the modern world. Down the stone paved sidewalk an old man hobbles, seemingly older than a few of the historic houses; his long beard grizzled from age.

As other people pass him by, he waves his hand with a friendly, grandfatherly smile and a fiery spark in his eyes. When a few turn back to look at the old man again, they find that he has vanished without a trace.

John Brown was fifty-nine when he was hung, for in sighting slave revolts and for the deaths of five slave holders from the Pottawatomie Massacre in May of 1856 that were killed by him and his men. The massacre was part of the collection of historical events now called

"Bleeding Kansas".

He was captured during the raid at Harpers Ferry, during which Brown and eighteen of his followers attacked the Harpers Ferry Armory. His plan was to seize the weapons in the large armory and hand them out to arm the local slaves and incite a large revolt.

The raid began on October 16th, 1859; on October 19th, the armory, which quickly became known as John Brown's fort, was surrounded by United States marines under the command of Colonel Robert E. Lee. It only took three minutes for the marines to capture Brown and his raiders. In the brief fight between the military and the raiders, ten of the raiders were killed, including Brown's sons: Watson and Oliver. Five escaped, one of which was his son Owen; and eight, including Brown, were captured.

Brown's execution took place on December 2nd, 1859; causing a shock wave to spread throughout the country. Both North and South, the people's feeling were mixed as to whether they viewed Brown as a hero, villain, or someone who was just insane. His actions at Harpers Ferry caused a tidal wave that he could never have seen coming. Tensions between the North and South were already high, and with the added fear of slave revolts occurring because of the actions of abolitionist like John Brown, the frayed thread between the states finally broke.

South Carolina succeeded from the Union on December 20, 1860; followed by: Mississippi, Florida, Alabama, Georgia, Louisiana, Texas, Virginia, Arkansas, Tennessee, North Carolina, Missouri and finally Kentucky on November 20th, 1861..

The Hells of War:

Andersonville Prison

Georgia

and

Rock Island

Illinois

Ghosts are the luminescent glow of the candle of life; not as bright as the flame of life and not as black as the infinite darkness and death. The candle remains extinguishable at a moment's notice, yet it is powerful enough to stand against the suffocating silence of the night.

In the fog one can see them, hollowed shells of men stumbling across the poisoned earth. They wait, hoping for a release, an escape, from the prison shackles that not even death can severe.

Death is terrifying and it is intriguing, a mysterious manifestation of shadows, darkness and the unknown; what it is not is evil. Evil lies in the hearts of some men; evil is the manner of which some are forced to meet their early demises. Death is the end to their suffering and death alone does not create ghosts. Ghosts can be created by humans who are left with matters unsettled, the dead who do not know that they are dead, or by the deceased who are waiting for someone or something in order to pass on. Paranormal occurrences can be caused by ghosts, spirits or energy; energy that has been enriched and empowered by extremely emotional events trapped in time. Energy that has manifested in one of the darkest reaches of Hell in the Civil War.

"Can this be hell?" - prisoner at Andersonville.

An aura of darkness lies within the still walls of Andersonville prison; there is a heaviness and eeriness that makes some visitors have to leave after a short period of time within the walls. While there are reports of phantom sightings in the prison when there is a light fog touching the ground; paranormal activity is not all ghosts and apparitions, it can manifested energy in a place can cause an apprehension that can be felt by even the most skeptical of visitors.

Andersonville is a name that has become synonymous with the horrors of war; a dark tragedy that could have been prevented or stopped many times over. The name Andersonville was not the name of the prison in the beginning, originally it was Camp Sumter in Andersonville, Georgia.

When Camp Sumter opened in February of 1864, the stockade was built to house 10,000 Union prisoners. In fourteen months, the number of prisoners within the camp grew to 45,000. When the prisoners were transferred out in 1865, nearly 13,000 had died there.

As it was in other soldier's camps free and outside the prison walls, disease was rampant and a typical part of soldier life: scurvy, gangrene, among others, made their way through the ranks. The aspects that made Andersonville so much worse than other camps was the abuse, violence, starvation and executions that happened in the compound.

After the closing of Andersonville, pictures were circulated of skeletal men who did not look like they should even be alive. The North blamed these horrors on Captain Henry Wirz, the commander of Andersonville and he went to the gallows for his war crimes. In review of all the facts surrounding the deaths of the men within the prison, he was just as much of a scapegoat as a criminal. Of course the prisoners were starving to death, that is true, their Confederate guards were also going hungry. The prison opened in February of 1864, Union General Sherman and his infamous, "march to the sea" and the Atlanta campaign began in May of 1864, during which, Atlanta was burned. Atlanta is 141 miles from Andersonville. With food already becoming a scarce commodity in the

South, an overcrowded prison was doomed to suffer especially in Georgia which was distress from other attacks by the North.

The overcrowding is an issue that could have been resolved, however, the exchange of prisoners had been stopped. There is a widely accepted misconception that the prisoner exchange was stopped by General Grant because the South would not parole any African American soldiers captured. However, by accounts of other Union prisoners of war trapped in the South, most freed slaves were either sent back to their masters or used by the Confederate army for work. With President Lincoln stating that for every Union prisoner executed, a Southern prisoner would be as well, kept a lot of executions at bay. The more reasonable answer is that the North was not willing to send Rebel prisoners back to the South in order to once again join their comrades on the battlefield. As word spread about the treatment of Northern prisoners, they would not have been good for any continued fighting for the Union cause anyway.

Executions did still happen within the walls of Andersonville. There was a line set up in the stockade and if a prisoner crossed it he was to be shot on sight. Several men went to their deaths in this manner, choosing the mercy of the bullet over starvation.

The lack of provisions caused some men to become a mob of villains, robbing their fellow prisoners of food, clothing and blankets; afterwards leaving them to die, at least most of the time. There were murders within those prison walls and no man can hide from justice forever. Fed up with their fellow Union soldiers causing as much harm as their Confederate guards, the prisoners rallied together, and met violence with justice. The Andersonville Raiders had between 200 and 400 members, against the thousands of sickly prisoners that they deprived. With the permission of Captain Wirz, the prisoners held a trial for the leaders of the raiders. On July 11, 1864, the six leaders of the raiders: Willie Collins, John Sarsfield, Charles Curtis, W.R. Riekson, Patrick Delaney, and A. Munn were hung from a gallows that was built within Andersonville's walls made just for them.

The graves of the six raiders are set apart from the other 13,737 graves in Andersonville cemetery. Every Memorial Day, flags are placed on 13,731 of the graves of our honored dead, 1,040 of which are unknown; the raiders graves are left untouched and undecorated, taking their disgrace beyond the grave.

Andersonville was the pit of Hell for the South. A horrid stain on the Confederacy that showed the darkness that can hide in men. It was a horrible place to be, but it is only fair to admit that the North had their own pit at Rock Island, Illinois.

Rock Island Prison

Murdered! This one word describes the potential fate of prisoners at Rock Island Prison. Relations between the guards of Andersonville and its prisoners were vastly different from the Union guards and its captives. While Andersonville prisoners were shot for crossing the dead line, which some did just to avoid starvation; men at Rock Island were shot for no reason at all.

Charles Wright of Tennessee kept a diary of his life at Rock Island. He arrived at Rock Island prison on January 16th, 1864. Sometimes, justice can only be served an event when hearing the words from those who were there:

"May 12, 1864.- Ordered, that no prisoner be out of his barracks after "taps."

May 13, 1864.- Ordered, any prisoner shouting or making a noise will be shot.

1864

April 27- Prisoner shot by sentinel.

May 27- One man killed and one wounded in the leg.

June 9- Franks, Fourth Alabama Cavalry, killed last night at barrack No. 12. He was shot by the sentinel on the parapet as he was about to step into the street. His body fell into the barrack, and lay there till morning. The men afraid to go near him during the night.

22- Bannister Cantrell, Co. G., 18th Georgia, and James W. Ricks, Co. F., 50th Georgia, were shot by the sentinel on the parapet. They were on detail working in the ditch, and had stopped to drink some fresh water just brought to them.

26- Prisoner shot in leg and arm while in his bunk at barrack

September 26- William Ford, Co. D, Wood's Missouri Battery, of barrack 60, killed by sentinel on the parapet. He was returning from the sink, and shot through the body at the rear of barrack 72.

26- T. P. Robertson, Co. I, Twenty-fourth South Carolina, shot by sentinel on parapet, and wounded in the back, while sitting in front of barrack 38, about 8 o'clock this morning.

26- T. J. Garrett, Co. K, Thirteenth Arkansas, shot by sentinel on parapet during the night while going to the sink.

27- George R. Canthew, of barrack 28, shot by sentinel on parapet.

28- Sentinel shot into barrack No. 12 through the window".

Wright was paroled on October 21st.

With so many murders, it would not be surprising if one of the shadows seen passing through the halls is one of the many victims seeking justice or retribution for their killers.

ANTIETAM
Maryland

"It is the most haunted house I have ever been in". - Paranormal Investigator on the Pry House at Antietam

Anything and everything became makeshift field hospitals, both during and after the battles: hastily built tents, citizen's homes, barns, businesses, if a place had any sort of shelter to it, it became a hospital. These hastily constructed hospitals offered the soldiers little besides pain and disease. Some soldiers would have preferred death on the battlefield to being carried to a field hospital.

"She had seen wagons coming up the hill, full of wounded men. And measuring to her shoulder on her outstretched arm she said, 'The blood is running out of them that deep!' This horrible picture sent us flying to town...We worked right on the street and sidewalk to comfort the men as hospitals were created". - Mary Bedinger Mitchell (Shepherdstown, Maryland Resident who was eleven years old during the battle of Antietam)

Sterilization was rarely a consideration; the thought of transmittable diseases and germs could hardly be a concern at such a time. Bodies would be laid close together to make room for more wounded. The fit or slightly injured would carry in the badly wounded and dying. Dining rooms tables would become operating tables. Blood would fall upon and stain the wooden floor boards in people's houses and in some cases, the blood stains still remain.

"It was the (St. Peter's) Lutheran Church's parsonage. After the battle it was used as a hospital, the floors were stained with blood. My great-grandmother had attempted to remove the stains, got them to go away and then the next day they were back, she eventually just covered them all up with rugs. Which then I believe she said had soaked up the stains and then were on the rugs as if they were wet". - descendant of Antietam Resident

The Pry House

The sounds of surgeries and suffering from long past still reside in the Phillip Pry Farm House. Immediately before the fighting at Antietam and during the battle, the house of Phillip Pry served as headquarters for Union Commander General George B. McClellan. It was quite common for high ranking generals to usurp someone's home as a headquarters for themselves.

After McClellan, the house also served as a headquarters for Medical Director Dr. Jonathan Letterman. Thanks to Letterman and his progressive mind, the Pry House is considered the birthplace of emergency and military medicine. Some of what Letterman did is still used today. The house offers self-guided tours, giving investigators a chance to turn on a digital recorder away from other people, and on a slow traffic day, the house offers many glimpses into the past.

During a walkthrough of the downstairs of the house on September 7, 2012, ten days before the 150th anniversary of the battle, a digital recorder picked up the sounds of a man screaming in such pain that it could only be figured that he was having a limb amputated.

A woman can also be heard saying, *"ghastly"* or *"nasty wounds, can you help him?"*
Walking up the stairs, another female spirit can be heard, *"The power of Christ gives me strength...."*

A woman in 19th century dress has been seen in the house by several people: including one of the paranormal investigators of the Black Moon Paranormal Society who saw the bottom half of a 19th century dress colored in black. Others who have seen the woman include firefighters who were fighting a blaze in the house in the 1970s and saw a woman standing in a second floor window, after the second floor had already collapsed.

Most of the documentation of paranormal events in the house began after the fire, which burned about a third of the house. Workers repairing the building afterwards also saw the woman standing in the window before work had been done to replace the floor. After the repair workers saw her in the window, and then later coming down the staircase in full-body apparition form, they quit and another crew had to be hired to finish the job. The window that the woman has been repeatedly seen standing in front of is in the room where General Israel Bush Richardson died after he was wounded during the battle of Antietam; leading many to believe that the apparition is that of his wife, "Fannie", who cared for him after his injury until his death on November 3rd, 1862. Richardson's sister, Marcella, also cared for the dying general.

During the years following the war, when the Pry family still owned the house, the household children refused to go into the room where the general died. So that was where Mrs. Pry would hide the sweets.

Other voices have been picked up in the house, some possibly relating to the battle and the usurping of the house, and then there are other voices that are a little more unexplainable. Most of the accounts and voices heard are residual, meaning that the ghosts will not answer your questions or communicate with you, because they are trapped in their own time and oblivious to the changes around them. They are more along the lines of an historical energy footprint, though not every ghost in the house is unaware of their living visitors.

*Investigation September 7th, 2012 at 12:18p.m. * Walking through the two rooms downstairs by the front door and at the bottom of the stairs.*

12:25:28 p.m.– EVP – "But the ring!" – female voice

12:25:40p.m. – EVP – "I found it".

12:26:17 p.m. – EVP – "Give out my key?" – female voice, with a slight sob on the word key.

12:26:54 p.m. – Investigator – Sees shadow behind surgery display in downstairs room.

12:27:54 p.m. – EVP – male screaming

*Walking up the staircase

12:30:44 p.m. – EVP – "The power of Christ gives me strength…" – female voice.

12:30:59 p.m. – EVP – "Sarah, sweet Sarah, _____, sweet Sarah". – male voice singing

12:31:45 p.m. – EVP – Roaring scream that sounded as though someone was being operated on. (Anesthetics were rarely used during the war).

Boot prints have been heard walking up and down the stairs and on the front porch by past occupants of the house. Before it was a museum it was occupied by the Park Service, first as storage and then as a residence. The Pry family sold the house and moved to Tennessee in 1873; even with receiving money from the government, the family was never able to recruit the thousands of dollars they lost during the war from their crops and livestock being eaten, stolen or destroyed. Only after the deaths of Philip and Elizabeth Pry, were they able to return home to the Antietam area; their bodies were entered into the Keedysville cemetery. Although it seems as if Mrs. Pry has also returned to her home after death.

As we left the house that day, reaching for the door handle to leave, a male voice cries out, *"come back and help"*. An intelligent ghosts, trapped in another time, waiting for more people to come and help the dying.

Dunker Church

The original Dunker Church that stood as witness to the battle of Antietam no longer exists. After the battle, the church was repaired; by the turn of the century, it was a weak structure near collapsing. In 1921, following a storm, the church crumbled to the ground. The structure that stands now was built as a symbol of peace for the 100th anniversary of the battle in 1962. Original materials were used in the construction and it was built on top of the foundation of the old church.

During the battle, heavy fighting occurred here between Union forces and the Confederate left flank. Photographs taken after the battle show dead bodies lying on the grounds of the church. According to historical documents, it was used as a temporary medical station and a Union embalming station.

Visitors to the church have reportedly heard the phantom sounds of cannon fire.

Investigation September 7th, 2012 at 10:30am at the Dunker Church
 10:31:24 a.m. – EVP – "Careful"
 10:32:37 a.m. – EVP – Cannon blast sound

Bloody Lane

Few military units are as well-known or as revered as the Irish Brigade. The formation, history and involvement of the Brigade during the Civil War is interesting enough for an entire book solely on them. The first regiment was the "Fighting 69th" New York. It originally was made up of New York regiments, and later, as the war progressed other regiments joined the ranks: the 116th Pennsylvania and the 29th Massachusetts, which was replaced by the 28th Massachusetts after the battle of Antietam.

The Irish Brigade served the Union and Irish-Americans in other ways besides battle. One of the reasons for the formation of an ethnic unit was to show their fellow Americans that they too were united together for the country and that the wave of immigrants coming in because of the famine in Ireland should be viewed as equals to the rest. Irish support for the Union cause hinted at a warning to Britain whom supported the Confederacy. The soldiers in the Irish Brigade were ferocious in battle, numerous historical reports remarked on their courage and stamina. Their well-known Irish war cry, *"faugh a ballagh"*, translated to *"clear the way"* is still heard by visitors to Antietam to this very day.

During the battle, the Irish Brigade found themselves marching throw Miller's Field to come face to face with the center of the Confederate line entrenched on the old sunken road. The Irish began an assault on the road, buying time for supporting troops to come in and break the Confederate position. The cost for the Irish was a loss of 60% of their force, wounded, dead or missing and; the old farm road being renamed the "Bloody Lane".

It was on a hunch during the investigation of the Bloody Lane that I found that the Irish still haunt the road. *"Dia duit, ta mo ainm Shannon. Cad is ainm duit?"* I asked. *"Hello, my name is Shannon. What is your name?"* The reply was, *"Michael"*. He stated his last name as well; however it was not clear enough to hear it.

Several Michael's are listed on the roster for the Brigade, a man by the name of Michael Hanlon of Company D of the Irish Brigade died during the battle of Antietam, he was twenty years old. There is a possibility that it was a non-Irish Brigade ghost who understood that I was introducing myself and answered accordingly without knowing the language. The following circumstances, do not make me believe that idea.

As I walked to the brigade's monument to take a picture, the digital recorder picked up the words, *"Ta go maith"*, Irish for, *"I am good"*; followed by another unreadable word that started with a *"B"*. The man who spoke was calm and collected as he spoke, not a trace of fear or forlorn in his voice. By his words, he seems rather content to remain where one can only assume he died courageously in battle.

Burnside's Bridge

While fighting and dying were happening on one side of the battlefield, Union troops were trying to cross a stone bridge; later known as Burnside's Bridge, after Union Major General Ambrose E. Burnside. After crossing the bridge, the Union troops took the hill on the other side of the bridge, driving the Confederate's back to Sharpsburg, Maryland. Burnside would have continued his assault, but was stopped due to the arrival of Confederate Major General A.P. Hill's division from Harpers Ferry.

Paranormal activity around the bridge was quiet on the day we visited. The only spirit that had anything to say was a comment of, "no" when asked if he liked the hat (a Union kepi) that one of the investigators was wearing as a trigger object. Trigger objects are items connected to that time period or person that can be used to invoke a stirring of energy in the spirit world. Many different objects can be used, when investigating places connected to the Civil War consider: loose leaf tobacco, replica clothing, old bullets, etc. Any of these may "trigger" a response.

The battle of Antietam could technically be considered a Union victory. Confederate General Robert E. Lee ordered his troops back across the Potomac River into Southern territory; which left the town in Union hands. Overall, the battle is considered a draw. When the war ended several years later in 1865, Antietam, one of the earliest battles of the war, would be marked as the single bloodiest day of the war, with an estimated total of 23,000 men dead, wounded or missing.

CHICKAMAUGA
GEORGIA

Lantern light flickered in the darkness, as if stars were glowing on the earth. Tears welled in her eyes, streaming down her wet cheeks, blurring the flickering glow of the lantern's light. She sucked in a sob as she almost stepped on the body of a man, his gray coat ripped by a bullet hole. Lifting her skirts, she walked around him saying the Lord's Prayer. More bloated, deformed bodies lay before her, surrounding her in a never ending sea of corpses.

Through the darkness, the glimmer of more lanterns blurred before her eyes; other widows of the South, her sisters in misery, searching for their lost loves. Under the lantern's glow, she found a familiar face and collapsed to her knees in a welling of grief, her cries echoing into the night.

The battle of Chickamauga lasted two days. It was the last major victory of the Confederate Army and the second bloodiest battle of the war; with Gettysburg being the first. By the end of this battle in Northwest Georgia , 34,624 men were listed as causalities, 16,170 for the North and 18,454 for the South. A harrowing blow to the forces of both sides who were still licking their wounds from Gettysburg .

The glowing lanterns are a part of the stories that are repeated on most battlefields, wives and mothers searching for lost family members. Most eye witness accounts center on two apparitions: the so-called "bride or lady in white" and an account of a Confederate soldier. The Confederate soldier is seen along one of the roads that runs along the battlefield, he is almost a menacing presence warning people away from the place that saw so much bloodshed. Or perhaps he is warning people away because of a legend that is older than the Civil War itself. That is the legend of 'Ol' Green Eyes', who is either a haunted creature dating back to a time when Native Americans inhabited the area, or "it" is the ghost of a headless Confederate soldier. If he is a headless soldier, he would be the second one on the battlefield since there is a tale that has circulated about the specter of a headless horseman.

As for the lady in white, which is the nickname I prefer to call her by, she is seen both day and night wandering the battlefield searching for her lost betrothed. Undoubtedly many a betrothed or newly wedded man met his end on that battlefield, so there is a chance that at least some part of story is true. Yet, there are other factors to consider when speaking of claims of the paranormal; such as could the man's intended bride appear on the battlefield after her own death to search for him? The answer to that question depends on whether or not a person believes that ghost can travel. I believe that the answer to this question is yes. There have been experiences at other places that lead me to believe that after a person's body dies their spirit is then free to: travel back to their home, remain where they are, or go in search of something or someone that was precious to them. Another theory is that ghost can haunt the place or person that is responsible for their death, which in this instance would be one of the romanticized cases of heartbreak.

(This theory does not account for those ghosts who are trapped in whatever place and cannot leave but, under that idea there lays many possibilities as to why they cannot leave the place. Perhaps they do not know that they are dead, another ghost is holding them back, they have unfinished business in said location, they feel that they deserve to be trapped where they are or it is a residual haunt. There are probably plenty more reasons as to why certain ghosts remain, each can have their own individual reason, but you get the idea).

While the tradition of wearing a white wedding dress came about over twenty years before the war, when Queen Victoria of England married Prince Albert of Saxe-Coburg, most women were still carrying on the previous tradition of wearing whatever dress they had available. The color of the dress was not of the utmost importance. In a time before department stores, when most women maintained only a small wardrobe, this would have been the most practical idea. This brings to account the question of, 'is the woman in white really wearing a wedding dress'?

Most eye witness accounts say it is a white dress, which could just be the color of the aura of the apparition. It would not be unusual for a full body apparition to have a white glow to it or to, in other cases, take the form of a shadow.

There is another less spoken of possibility as to why a woman is roaming the battlefield. After the battle it was found that one of the Union dead was a teenaged female who had disguised herself to fight for the cause. If this female is the woman seen haunting the battlefield, since she died in Union and appears in a dress; it would give evidence to the idea that ghost can change their appearance after death to what suits them. If that is true, then quite possibly what we have here is an intelligent haunt. Despite the numerous accounts, no one has yet been able to ask her who she is and why she is there.

Slowly she drifts across the battlefield of Chickamauga . Searching the ground that once carried thousands of dead bodies for the one she lost. She glows like a white luminescent candle held in another dimension. A veil shields her face and her white dress swirls around her feet in flowing waves. She is unaware that the world is drifting by around her, changing while she is trapped in a world of her own far apart from ours. In sorrow she walks with a heavy heart for while love is immortal, our bodies are not.

Directions: 3370 LaFayette Rd , Fort Oglethorpe

The Southern Belle of
CHOWAN UNIVERSITY
NORTH CAROLINA

(McDowell Columns Building)

    Leaves swept through the grand entry way of the old fashioned styled plantation house. Outside the main doors, white columns lifted to the sky; white rocking chairs lined the porch under the roof. The door shut quietly behind the cloaked figure. She glided down the staircase, her feet never touching the ground. Her movements smooth and fluid, as she crossed the park of trees in the center of the campus, known as " Squirrel Park ". Her white dress flowed in the grand appearance of a Southern Belle, brown flowers were embroidered across the bottom. A brown cloak wrapped tightly around her shoulders against the cloak. She neared one of the bench swings and then the Brown Lady disappeared.

    The version I saw of the Brown Lady is not like others have recorded in the past. They say she wears a brown dress, as far as I can say that is not true. When I saw her, she was wearing a glowing white dress, with a delicate, ornate brown embroidery at the bottom; over top she wears a brown cloak a lighter shade than her dark hair.

I only saw her once, strolling from the Columns building, the large white plantation house in the center of the campus. Through the park she strolled. Curiously I followed the direction I saw her walk to and disappear as I was sitting on one of the swinging benches in the work. Shortly after I saw her disappear I felt an impression in my back. Startled by the unexpected touch, I hurried inside to find the indentation of a finger nail in my shoulder. I was not alone, the person with me would not have been able to make the same mark.

Nearly every student who attended Chowan College knew the story of the Brown Lady. There are different variations, some say she died of sickness of Halloween night, years after the Civil War. This oddly coincidental ghost story is usually recounted by those who did not attend the school. Most students tell the story that she was engaged to a Confederate soldier who died during the war; upon hearing the news of his death she jumped from the roof of the McDowell Columns building, an exquisitely large, white plantation house that once served as rooms for the girls who attended the school. The rest will say that she died of a broken heart after hearing of his death.

Certain events of the story are possible; unlike a few other schools, Chowan remained open during the Civil War. When Chowan first opened in 1848, it was the Chowan Baptist Female Institute; the McDowell Columns building was built in 1851 to house the students. In 1910, the school became Chowan College and began accepting male students in 1931. Because of the Great Depression, the school closed in 1937 and did not reopen until 1992. Finally, in 2006, the school became a university.

Several ghostly tales made their way around campus, especially on the third floor of the Belk building. Various noises and eye witness accounts have been told over the years, however, none of those are related to the Civil War.

Directions: Murfreesboro, North Carolina

CORINTH
MISSISSIPPI

Horse's hooves pounded the ground in a frenzy. The distinctive clang of drawn sabers striking together above the snorting of the horses. Blades of grass trampled under the hooves, leaving impressions in the grass.

The riders yelled, shouting in their adrenaline rushed aggression feud. A swirling tornado of dust kicked up around the coats of blue, gray and brown; covering everything it touched. churning with the dust, a light fog rolled in, shielding the bottom halves of the cavalry's from view.

As the fog was carried away by the wind, the phantom cavalry travelled with it. Ghost riders spurring their horses forward to the next battlefield.

-Narrative of a re-enactors account of what they heard at Corinth Battlefield. A similar tale has also been told at Ball's Bluff Battlefield in Virginia.

Much of the landscape around Corinth Battlefield remains the same. A tiny town amongst streams, forest, hills and open farmland. The battlefield is a mere shadow compared to the battle of Shiloh, which is tied to Corinth in proximity and the time to the larger battle.

In 1862, the town was under siege by Union troops that were considered to be well-entrenched. The men were prepared to hold their position at the key railroad junction at the town.

Meanwhile, in Tennessee, the battle of Shiloh erupted in April of 1862. Soldiers remarked that after the battle of Shiloh, the sweet adventure of war was turning old and the readiness to fight was lost.

THE OLD
CREEKSIDE INN
PENNSYLVANIA

I was just a young girl when my family first purchased the old Creekside Inn. It was a decrepit shell of its former glory. I still remember the dust and grim that covered every floor of the building, the piles of beer cans in the rooms and cigarette ash encrusted pool tables. My family were not strangers to historic inns in need of rehabilitation, even if this one was worse off.

As my family spent their days cleaning and scrubbing every room from top to bottom I stayed in a makeshift play room in one of the cleaner apartment rooms. I would read, watch tv on an old set with giant knobs that had to be turned on and off manually. My days were spent by myself, though I never felt as if I was alone. In an age when I still believed in fairy godmothers and imaginary friends, it was not until I was older that I actually understand what my sixth sense was telling me.

Once the inn was clean, my afternoons were no longer spent entertaining myself in a little room and I rarely spent any long periods of time in the building at all. Not until I was thirteen and living in recently renovated apartment in the second floor. This time around I held a better understanding of the mysteries and horrors around me. Footsteps would walk up and down the stairs. Cigar smoke would billow down from the third floor, that one was at least explainable by the scent being released by the old wooden boards in the house. There was also the feelings of being watched with such intensity that I was afraid to look into mirrors because I was afraid of what I would see behind me; the dog would bark at nothing, at night I would hear men and horses outside.

A few times in my inexperienced youth I tried using an ouija board, all it told me was that there were skeletons in the basement. The basement was a disgusting, disturbing place. Even someone without a hint of psychic awareness would be wary in such a place. Some days, to test my courage I would take the staircase down into the darkness. Darkness that hid a tunnel beneath the inn that led to the creek that was used by escaped slaves on their trek to freedom. Most parts of the tunnel had caved in years before. It never took long before I would lose my nerve and run back up the stairs, hearing the stomping of boots running behind me, chasing me up the stairs.

Eventually the strange dreams began, a runaway slave dressed in torn and tattered clothing came into my room, pointing into the darkness towards the creek and bridge. "Stay away from the lights" he said. Looking out the window, I could see the glow of lantern lights in the distance moving towards the inn.

After the night I had the dream, the strange noises and feelings continued until, at last, one of them came to form. One night I came home late, I do not remember the date and walked into my room to find the full body apparition of a Confederate soldier curled in a fetal position on my bed. He looked as though he was in intense pain, a light mist whisked around him. After a few seconds he disappeared.

What is surprisingly, there were Confederate troops near the location of the inn. The main battle may have been in Gettysburg, but the troops moved beyond the town. Incidents of soldier occupation were at: Chickies Rock, Cashtown, Chambersburg and York Haven.

Confederates were moving through York Haven to two bridges that ran across the Conewago Creek, the same creek that the inn sits beside. Adding to the already fantastic history on a old roadside inn whose one deed dates back to the 1860s, but there are stories that Charles Dickens and the Marquis de Lafayette both stayed at the inn in the 1820s and 1840s.

The old Creekside Inn still exists under a different name, it still serves the public as a wayside inn and most will never know the mysterious, darker side the lays waiting in the basement or the escaped slave who lived in fear of his life or the Confederate soldier who may have died within those walls.

Franklin

Tennessee

A gold embroidered four leaf clover adorned his kepi. The handsome figure of a man with a neatly trimmed brown beard paced the balcony of the Carnton Plantation. Back and fourth, he paced, stopping to peer into the distance. Impatiently General Patrick Cleburne, "the Stonewall of the West", began pacing again. The troubled Irishman could not understand why word was not coming about his division. Crossing over to grip the railing, he looks out over the fields in front of the Carnton Plantation, and fades away.

General Cleburne's body was found on December 1, 1864, fifty yards from the Union line. His lifeless corpse was carried by ambulance to be placed on the back porch of the plantation, along with the bodies of three other Confederate generals: John Adams, Hiram Granbury and Orbit Strahl. Cleburne was buried in Ashwood Cemetery in Tennessee, at the former President James K. Polk's family plot. His body was moved six years later to Maple Hill Cemetery in Helena, Arkansas; his adopted hometown after he emigrated from Ireland. Buried with him in Ashwood Cemetery, at St. John's Episcopal Church at the time were also: Brigadier General H.B. Granbury, Brigadier General O.P. Strahl and Brigadier General S. R. Gist; two of the generals whose bodies had lain next to his on the Carnton Plantation's back porch.

Survivors of the battle of Franklin remembered the event as horrifying, in the words of General Stewart it was, "the most furious and desperate battle of the war in the West"; another veteran said, "Franklin was the grave of the Army of Tennessee". Historians have argued about the haste and carelessness that General John Bell Hood had thrown his army into battle. Some will say that he was determined to stop the Union force led by Major General John M. Schofield.

Whether it was through haste or determination, the missteps of the Confederate army at Franklin Battlefield during the second battle of Franklin; the loss was crippling. The "Pickett's Charge" of the West, began with approximately 20,000 men.

During the battle: Generals for the Confederate Army: Six killed or mortally wounded, seven wounded and one was captured. Regimental Commanders: Fifty-five casualties. Soldiers: 1,750 killed, 3,800 wounded, 702 missing/captured. Compared to 189 killed in the Union Army. The Battle of Franklin essentially destroyed the Army of Tennessee.

The Carnton Plantation

Part of the common knowledge of the second battle of Franklin is a lady known as the Widow of the South. Carrie Winder McGavock was the mistress of Carnton Plantation, a white Greek Revival plantation with two story porches in the front and back of the house. Her husband, John McGavock, was the son of the man who built the plantation in 1825. John died in 1893.

After the battle, Carnton became the largest hospital in the area. Carrie tended to at least three hundred wounded. At least 100 men died in the plantation house, their blood staining the floors. Her children's bedroom was turned into an operating room and by morning after the first night it is said that Mrs. McGavock's skirts were soaked in blood at the bottom. By the time the battle came to her home, all the slaves they had owned were gone

Her tenderness to the soldiers who were wounded in battle only a mile from her home is why she was called the Widow of the South. She cooked breakfast for them, tended to their wounds and watched hundreds die.

General Hood was unwilling to see his men buried in mass graves. As General Schofield left his wounded and dead on the field and marched on to Nashville, Hood gave orders that all the men should be buried by their name, rank and unit. Many of these graves were located on the property of the Carter House, which is located near the plantation and was witness to the heat of battle.

Shortly after the war, the Widow of the South and her husband donated two acres of their property for the graves of the soldiers. With the help of the citizens of Franklin raising funds, every soldier was transferred into the McGavock Confederate Cemetery with new tombstones, ones that would not rot away within a few years.

All the names were entered into a book that was kept by Carrie and still remains in the plantation. Time has worn away the names on nearly 600 graves, over 700 remain readable, and not forgotten.

The Carter House

His breath came in heavy pants; just beyond the ridge he could see home. Smoke billowed through the chimney of the modest brick farmhouse on the chilly November day. Quietly, he crept between the trees, darting behind one; he laid his back against the rough bark, his eyes glancing around every tree looking for a color of a navy blue coat. Seeing the way clear he ran to the garden gate that lay between the smokehouse and the farm office, pausing just for a minute.

Frantic movement ahead caught his eye, seeing a loving familiar face frantically waving him away. His eyes darted around again, with a heavy sigh; he turned back the way he came, creeping into the wooded lands near the farm. Hurrying back to where his friend stood waiting for him, not bearing to see his family home overrun by Union soldiers, Tod Carter returned to where the Confederate Army was preparing for battle. Riding his gray horse, Rosencrantz, into battle, he shouted, "Follow me boys, I'm almost home!"

Theodrick 'Tod" Carter did make it home one last time, dying in his bed on December 2, 1864 from his wounds that he had received during what was to be called the battle of Franklin. He had been shot 100 feet from his family home. A tragic end to the son of Fountain Branch

Carter.

Earlier in the war, Tod had been a prisoner of war. Captured during the Battle of Missionary Ridge in 1863, he had been sent to Johnson's Island in Ohio. During a prisoner transfer from Johnson's to Point Lookout, Tod Carter jumped from a moving train to make his escape. With the help of a sympathetic Union family, Tod was able to make it back to Tennessee to find the armies meeting on his doorstep.

The house was built in 1830 by Fountain Branch Carter, who had purchased the 19 acres that the farm sat on in October of 1829. By the time of the battle, the farm had flourished but on November 30th of that year, Carter, his family and his farm found themselves in the middle to a battle that would span across two miles of land. On the day of battle, Union General Jacob D. Cox knocked on the Carter house door at 4:30 in the morning and took over the house to use as a Federal Command Post. Soldiers immediately clambered into the parlor and surrounding farmland, some slept, others dug entrenchments, and others tore down four barns and the family's cotton-gin for use of the timber.

At four in the afternoon, the battle began. The elder Carter took his family, servants and their neighbors, the Lotz family, and hid in the cellar. Twenty-three people huddled together in the cellar on the fateful day, twelve of them were children. A few Union soldiers tried to join the family out of fear of the battle but were quickly turned away. When the battle was finished, over a thousand bullet holes and the marks of a cannon ball riddled the small federal style brick farmhouse, leaving it the most bullet punctured house in America.

As night came, the family emerged from their haven to learn of the wounding of Tod by General Smith. His family went in search of him, finding him being carried to the house by two Alabamian soldiers. Tod Carter was buried in Rest Haven Cemetery.

A friend of mine visited the Carter House a few years ago and said that the house feels overlooked compared to the grand Carnton Plantation. In particularly when it comes to the paranormal, she felt an unexplainable eeriness in the house; a tenseness that she has not felt at other places.

There are reports from witnesses to activity in the house that believe that Tod Carter and his little sister Annie still reside in the house. Though charming and beloved in life, it is believed that it is his spirit causing some of the ill feelings in the home. Annie, on the other hand is young, spirited and playful; a contrast to her older brother. One should not be too harsh on Tod, after all he fought so hard against Northern soldiers and desperately to come home. Tod's final words before he died were, "home, home, home".

FREDERICKSBURG
VIRGINIA

"But out of that silence rose new sounds more appalling still; a strange ventriloquism, of which you could not locate the source, a smothered moan, as if a thousand discords were flowing together into a key-note weird, unearthly, terrible to hear and bear, yet startling with its nearness; the writhing concord broken by cries for help, some begging for a drop of water, some calling on God for pity; and some on friendly hands to finish what the enemy had so horribly begun; some with delirious, dreamy voices murmuring loved names, as if the dearest were bending over them; and underneath, all the time, the deep bass note from closed lips too hopeless, or too heroic to articulate their agony...It seemed best to bestow myself between two dead men among the many left there by earlier assaults, and to draw another crosswise for a pillow out of the trampled, blood-soaked sod, pulling the flap of his coat over my face to fend off the chilling winds, and still more chilling, the deep, many voiced moan that overspread the field."
-Joshua Lawrence Chamberlain: 20th Maine,
At the end of the first day's fighting at Fredericksburg,
"The Civil War Archive"

Marye's Heights, Fredericksburg

"Water", the words broke in a hoarse crack of a whisper. He struggled against the pain from the hole in his gut, lifting himself up on his elbows in the wet snow. Sweat soaked his brow despite the chill of the December air.

"Water!" The words screamed inside his head, again his voice cracked from dehydration. His vision clouded in a pain filled haze, a figure leaned over him; a halo of sunlight at his back, shadowing his face. The stranger touched a wet-rimmed canteen to the wounded mans chapped lips; the few drops of water bringing a wave of relief.

When the canteen was empty, the man crept away without a word moving on to the next man in need of relief. The wounded man stared blankly into the distance, watching the silent figure creep from man to *man before vanishing in a blur of sunlight reflecting off the snow, an earthly angel in gray.*

An angel did walk the fields of Fredericksburg on December 14th, 1862; his name was Sergeant Richard R. Kirkland. His tale has become a legend of the battle and he was hailed as the, "Angel of Marye's Heights".

The wailing of the wounded had seeped into the minds and hearts of those on the other side of the line, and for Kirkland it became too much to bear to stand back and do nothing as other human beings lay dying on the cold, hard ground.

After asking permission of his commanding officer, General Kershaw, Kirkland left the safety of the stonewall that he and his fellow South Carolinian's were positioned behind. They say that the guns on both sides were silent that day as Kirkland showed mercy to his "enemies". They say that the guns on both sides were silent that day as Kirkland showed mercy to his "enemies".

He would survive the battle of Fredericksburg, dying eight months later at the Battle of Chickamauga in Georgia; his last words were, "Save yourselves and please tell my Pa I died right". Kirkland's deeds would be forever remembered in the North and South and beyond.

EVP session September 3, 2011 10:20:07 a.m. –
Investigator - "Are there any soldiers here that Sergeant Kirkland tried to help and give water to?"
10:20:26 EVP - deep breath "three" or "me".

Some historians have questioned as to whether or not Sergeant Kirkland really did leap the stonewall at the Heights, his body covered in canteens that he borrowed from his fellow soldiers to give water to the wounded men in front of the stonewall. Contradicting a story that one ghost says was the truth. Kirkland never answered any of our pleas or questions directed at him and it is assumed that he does not linger in the place where he is known as a hero.

The Sergeant may no longer stomp the grounds of Fredericksburg but there is another hero who emerged on that day that still remains.

She was born Martha Farrow, throughout her life at one time or another she also had the last names of Innis and Stevens. During the battle of Fredericksburg she was called Martha Stevens. Her neighbors described her as being a strange woman; a bit too independent for the time period. She was living with a man by the name of Stevens, while her legal name was listed as Innis.

EVP session September 3, 2011 by the Innis House.
Investigator - "Is there anybody here?"
EVP - female voice - "Innis"

From her own accounts of the battle, Martha Stevens said that she cared for wounded soldiers. There is some debate as to what she actually did during the battle and some soldiers do not remember anything about the woman who claimed that she helped them. Whether or not she helped them in life, in death she still seems to linger with the soldiers who died on those cold December days.

~*~

Path at Fredericksburg that runs along the houses.

Investigation September 3rd, 2011, 10:12 am

We walked along a dirt path, tiny battle scarred buildings and the remains of foundations of houses that had seen the battle run along the road: the Stevens House, with its well; the Innis House and the Ebert House. Each of these places has a story to tell, written on the bullet holes that still mar the walls.

"Caught in a vortex of Union attacks against the Sunken Road", reads the plaque at the Stevens House. Confederate sharpshooters took their positions in the house, using the windows and roof to shoot at Union soldiers. Martha Stevens stayed in her home during the battle, braving (as she reported it) bullets flying all around her to retrieve water from her well and tear bandages off of her own clothing for the wounded soldiers. Her grave plot is near the house.

In between the Steven's and Innis' Houses, our electromagnetic field detector dropped from a average reading in the 60s down to the 40s, showing the fields in the area were low. Spikes to the EMF detector could have meant that paranormal activity was nearby.

By the Innis House
10:18:31am - Investigator - "What state are you from?"
10:18:37am - EVP - "Pennsylvania".
10:22:29am - EVP - "Away"

There were more than a few Pennsylvania regiments at Fredericksburg: the 69th, 71st, 72nd, 81st, 106th, 116th, 127th, 130th, 132th and the 145th Pennsylvania regiments are all listed as being at the battle.

Towards the end of the path is the Ebert House. Before the battle, the Ebert's were startled to find Union officers on their doorstep telling them to evacuate the home because of the impending battle. Days later, the family returned to find dead bodies strewn all over their property and their houses damaged by bullets.

By the Ebert House
10:27:14am - Investigator - "Are there spirits here that did not fight in the battle?"
10:27:31am - Investigator - "If so, what is your name?"

10:27:38am - EVP - "George".
10:28:14am - EVP - "House".
10:29:36am - Investigator's hand is touched where she is holding the digital recorder.

~*~

Fredericksburg National Battlefield is rather small in size compared to a few of the other battlefields within a few hours' drive of it. What is left is only a section of what was used by Union and Confederate troops would have used in December of 1862. Most of the area has built over, including areas that would have been used by soldiers while in camp.

Camp life was difficult; many men were leaving the comfort of their homes and families with warm hearths and home cooking in exchange for tents crowded with five to six men out in the elements. Rain, snow, heat, and the only shelter between the men and Mother Nature were stretches of cloth. Soldiers were forced at times to live off the land, picking fruit from trees, or in more desperate times, stealing from the local citizens.

A past resident of Fredericksburg passed this story on to me about an area that was part of the Confederate camp.

"Part of the Battle of Fredericksburg was conducted near what it now Benchmark Road in Sposty County. What is often forgotten is that Lee and his troops were camped there off of Benchmark and Mine Rd from after the Battle of Fredericksburg until Chancellorsville. So they spent many months between battles near the area. There is a very active haunting on that road and my mother and I have had several experiences with him. The most part of the story was when he decided to follow me home one day (my house is not haunted) when I was a junior in high school (I just graduated from college). I had been feeling him for some time on the road but then he decided to hang out in my bedroom". She continued with her story saying that her mother also felt the presence and told the man to leave the house, he did and never came back. Her story concluded with, "We still feel him from time to time on the road, although not every time we drive on it because we are on that road a lot". - Caitlin

The defeat at Fredericksburg was one of the most demoralizing losses for the Union..

FORT MCALLISTER
Georgia

There is quite a bit of skepticism when it comes to animal spirits. Even more-so than with human ones. Different theories have been presented on the case of animals coming back from beyond the grave and, as with people, the ideas fall into the categories of residual or intelligent.

Animals cannot answer prompted questions as to determine which category they will fall into, therefore the categories are based solely on opinions, usually by those closest to the pet and at times, even in war, a mascot.

Camp mascots are not unusual, dogs and horses were the most common. The 102nd Pennsylvania Infantry had a brown and white bull terrier named "Jack", the 69th New York Infantry had Irish Wolfhounds and the 1st Maryland had "Grace". Then there was General Robert E. Lee's horse Traveller and his hen, JEB Stuart's horse Virginia and "Stonewall" Jackson's horse Little Sorrell. Fort McAllister had a cat.

"Tom Cat" was a completely black feline and he was a cherished member of the garrison. During battle, he would run along the defenses. When he died on March 3rd, 1863 after being hit by a stray bullet, a report of the cat's death was forwarded on to General Beauregard.

Over a year later, the fort itself would also fall to the Union during Sherman's march to the sea. The end came on December 13, 1864, when 4,000 Union soldiers attacked McAllister and it's 230 defenders.

A phantom black cat is seen running around the area. Strangely, an all black cat has also been reportedly seen at Little Round Top in Gettysburg. Little Round Top is already believed by some ghost hunters to have a "vortex" that spirits can use to travel through; if so, that is quite a bit of traveling for a little cat.

Besides the phantom mascot, a headless Confederate officer who is said to be Major Gallie. Gallie's ghost has been seen since the 1960s, standing where he died.

Directions: 3894 Fort McAllister Road, Richmond Hill, GA 31324

FORT MIFFLIN
PENNSYLVANIA

William H. Howe was not what one would necessarily call an honorable soldier. Perhaps in death he is haunted by the final choices he made in life; the very same choices that led him to the gallows at Fort Mifflin on May 26th, 1864. It is believed that his ghost still roams the grounds, especially the cell he stayed in waiting on a pardon that never came. The story behind the ghost of Howe happened in the later years of the fort. So let us go back to the beginning.

Located on Mud Island on the Delaware River near Philadelphia , Fort Mifflin was commissioned by the British in 1771. Ironically, it would end up helping the American forces during the American Revolution a few years later. Over the course of five weeks in 1777, 400 Continental soldiers held off a barrage of cannon balls by the British Navy. In total, 10,000 cannon balls were fired on the fort, costing the Americans over 150 soldiers. Eventually, the Americans evacuated the fort, but not before General George Washington and the rest of the army were encamped at Valley Forge for the winter. It would not be until the spring of 1778 that the armies would meet again.

During the 1790s, the fort was rebuilt to repair the damage done during the Revolution in time for the War of 1812 when the Americans would again face the British army. In the 1860s, Fort Mifflin was used as a prisoner of war camp for the Civil War. While the main purpose was for housing Confederates, a few exceptions were made for traitors and deserters of the Union Army. The latter reason is how William Howe ended up at Mifflin.

Howe had joined the Union Army in time for the disastrous Union defeat in Fredericksburg, Virginia. Various genealogical and ancestry sites list his date of birth as being around 1839, which would have made him around the age of twenty-three at that battle. By all reports, he fought bravely during Fredericksburg, at the conclusion of which 1,284 of his fellow soldiers were dead, with another 9,600 wounded and 1,769 captured or missing. Howe was listed among the wounded, and between the wounds and a serious illness that had caught him, he left the army and went home to his wife.

When other Union soldiers came to arrest him to face the charges of desertion, he murdered one of them in his attempt to escape. The murder did not work to his benefit and only added to the charges against him. Two years and five months after the battle of Fredericksburg, Howe was hanged.

After the Civil War, the fort saw very little action. During World War I and World War II, it was used as an ammunition depot. The fort was owned by the United States Army until 1952, when it was turned over the city of Philadelphia.

Besides Howe, it is said that a screaming woman also haunts the fort. Differing reports dispute the name, however, most call her Elizabeth. Whoever she is, more than one person has recounted to me of hearing her chilling scream from inside the fort. The ghost of Jacob the blacksmith, also haunts the fort in the area of the Blacksmith's shop, making a racket as he toils away.

Twelve buildings still stand on the fort grounds: the Arsenal, Artillery Shed, Soldier's Barracks, Officer's Quarters, Commandant's House, West Sallyport, the Hospital, Casemates, East Magazine and Casemate 11. Casemates are enclosures used to shelter soldiers during attacks and prisoners during the Civil War. Of these buildings: the Officer's Quarters, the Blacksmith Shop and Casemate 11 are reportedly the most haunted.

Casemate 11 was discovered quite by accident in 2006. A caretaker was mowing the grass when his leg fell through a hole. After digging up the area, the cell was discovered and inside, carved into the stone wall, read the name 'William H. Howe'.

Directions: Fort Mifflin and Hog Island Roads, Philadelphia

GETTYSBURG
PENNSYLVANIA

Over a stretch of three days of battle, the Union (North) and Confederate (South) clashed in a sea of lead and bloody tides. Acres of Pennsylvania farmland were stained red with blood, the scent of death perfuming the air for months after the battle was over. Beneath our Northern soil thousands of men were buried, some without a name and many who considered the land to be enemy territory.

"While his body lies beneath the enemies soil at Gettysburg, we hope his spirit has passed to a better world where no enemy can hurt him again".

- Isaac M. Hite, Private in the Army of Northern Virginia

Gettysburg is considered by many to be the most haunted place in the United States. Hundreds of encounters and stories have been told and documented over the past century, ever since the battle ended. With a grand total of 51,000 causalities, there are plenty of ghost stories; some have yet to be told.

DAY 1

(July 1st, 1863)

Iverson's Pits

Early evening was setting in, the sun falling in a far away distance. Casting shadows on the ground, while the sky light up in color: pink, orange and blue. The fields were overgrown, high enough if a man crouched down to his knees he would not be seen. A beautiful scene for a picture. Several pictures were taken, a few simultaneously, others spaced out. Hours later, upon reviewing the pictures for touch ups the photographer found that in one of the photographs a light mist was in view of the camera lens. No other pictures had a mist, and she did not see the mist when she took the picture. It was just suddenly there and gone.

The Pits face the Eternal Light of Peace at Oak Hill. They were a slaughter pen where men died in formation, whole lines of men dead in their marching formations. In death, they were buried in those same lines in the pits where they died. Mass graves of men, without a tombstone to show their name. An area where paranormal activity could run rampant and it does.

Of all the areas on the battlefield, this one has one of the highest reports of phantom battle reenacts. Whole residual scenes involving many men in a bloody brawl to see who would be declared victor until the next battle.

Oak Hill

It was a cool evening in March of 2010, three friends chatted amiably while sitting on the walls around the Eternal Light Peace Memorial. They spoke of the battle, the soldiers and, of course, the ghosts. Taking turns in the growing dark to walk alone around the memorial and up a little trail behind it leading to a bare spot with new trees and no memorials. Being not yet spring, the area was not overgrown with the green brush that crowds beside the trail during the summer.

One of the females had gone first, she did not see or hear anything nevertheless she had the strange feeling of being watched. The male in the group went second, walking up the path behind them. As the two women sat on the wall watching the direction he had gone in when they noticed the shadowy figure of a man on the hill near where their friend had walked. As they watched the man, he began pointing towards Iverson's Pits and walked towards that part of the field. Thinking it was their friend pointing something out to them they turned to look in the direction he was pointing, seeing nothing, they turned back to find their friend coming towards them from the bottom of the trail he had gone up. The shadowy figure had been walking away from them in the

opposite direction.
There were no other cars or people in the area. The friends gathered their belongings and left the memorial.

Oak Hill is not a place that most people would know by name. That is because the area is better known by the monument that stands on its hallowed ground, the Eternal Light Peace Memorial.

May 15th, 2011

5:07:01 p.m. - Investigator - "Is Little Round Top over that way?"

5:07:06 p.m. - Digital Recorder - "Yes" – male voice.

DAY 2

(July 2nd, 1863)

Devils Den

In the early morning hours of a cold, wintry December day, myself and a friend began our first scientific based investigation and conversation with the dearly departed. Of all the areas in Central Pennsylvania, Gettysburg seemed to be the best to test our new equipment. Despite the heavy fighting and numerous soldiers that passed through the den on their way to their deaths, this area of the battlefield is relatively quiet when it comes to the paranormal.
At a small corner of the bolder mass, we received our first EVP on the digital recorder. Because of the scratchiness of the white noise, the wave lengths in which spirits sometimes speak, the young soldier's name was inaudible. When asked his age he responded with, "twenty-four give or take". Afterwards, the area grew silent again. A young age to be fated to eternity on the other side; yet, despite his early death, the fact that he was pleasant and was willing to answer our questions spoke volumes for the young man who has yet to be named.

Area of the famed "Sharpshooter", this is where we received the response of "24 give or take".

Only one other ghost communicated with us in the den area. He was near the parking lot in the front of the den; popping into our conversation about visiting the Wheatfield and telling us not to go there. His voice sounded much older and huskier than the guest of our previous conversation. Whether it was because he knew of the carnage in that field and the danger that once awaited there or because he did not want us to leave is unknown for afterwards he grew silent as well. It can take a lot of energy for the dead to try to communicate and many times we are left with only pieces of conversation and sentences, with many questions left unanswered.

On August 23rd, 2012, I received a message from someone who had taken a spirit box to the Devils Den area to see who, if anyone, would speak to them. The person did not ask any questions, he just let the box play and pick up what words were spoken. He received four: "Mama, John, Lincoln, Difficulty".

"We were ordered forward, and advanced a distance of one mile over a very rough and rugged road – the worst cliffs of rocks there could have been traveled over."

- Official report – Colonel James Sheffield, 48th Alabama . General Law's Brigade.

Devils Den is truly an amazing canvas of boulders and rocks. Below the watchful eyes of Little Round Top, a treacherous expanse of large boulders and stones lie as if they were placed there by unnatural forces; a puzzle of pieces piled together with little shadowy crevices where men crawled to hide from the torturous sun above and the hail of bullets surrounding them. The wounded and frightened were both seeking the same refuge together where some may still be seeking their escape from the battle outside. Unlike some other places on the battlefield, such as the Slaughter Pen and the Valley of Death , which earned their names because of the battle; the den came upon its name years before the war. Although no one knows for sure how or when it received such an ominous name, whether through tall tales or because of a Native American battle that happened long before the Civil War, the land has certainly lived up to it's title. No matter which, with having such a name, chances are there are more than just Civil War soldiers wandering through the boulders, the nearby stream, and the valley that has become overwhelmingly associated with death and blood.

Little Round Top

"Bayonets!", the command was shouted down the ranks of the 20th Maine. Bayonets or death was the unspoken truth. The young soldier glanced at his commander Colonel Joshua L. Chamberlain, gauging his reaction. Against the unfathomable odds and facing the cold steel of the enemy (an army created using friends, relatives, schoolmates and sometimes even neighbors of the Union army) his commander stood unflinching. Splinters of tree bark fluttered into his face as mini ball barely missing him. Transporting the young man back to the reality of the moment, he pulled the sharp bayonet from it's casing, mounting it on his musket.

"The rebs must be getting tired", said the older soldier next to him. His scruffy beard black from biting the gun powder packets.

Nodding at his comrade, the younger reclined against the tree where the splinters had spawned. Exhaling a deep breath. Watching as the line of men down from him stood in attention preparing to charge. On unsteady legs he rose with them. His heart beating faster as the rushes of adrenaline coursed through his mortal body. He took another deep breath, putting all his weight on his right legs preparing for the race down the hill.

The command came quick, sharp and loud, "charge!". In one fluid motion the line of blue moved down the hill.

Strange tales have been woven into this little battle ravaged hill. When asked about their experiences on the battlefield, a group of friends told the story of something that happened to them while visiting the location of Colonel Joshua L. Chamberlain's famous charge.

Chamberlain's charge has made quite a mark in history, when the commander of the 20th Maine was faced with the possible annihilation of his regiment and possibly the Union army due to being out of ammunition he ordered an unprecedented bayonet charge down the hill into the oncoming enemy. Many factors played into Chamberlain's decision, the fact that the Southerner's were exhausted from the long march into Gettysburg followed by repeated charges up the Little Round Top. That his regiment was the end of the Union line and if they fell then the South could sweep around behind the entire Union army and surround them.

Down the line from the Maine men, the 83rd Pennsylvania, 44th New York and 16th Michigan were facing the rest of General Hood's Division of the 4th and 5th Texas, and 4th and 47th Alabama regiments.

March 30th, 2012

3:30:10 p.m. - Investigator - "Are you a part of the 20th Maine ?"

3:30:15 p.m. - Spirit Box - "Yes"

3:13:20 p.m. - Investigator - "What is your name?"

3:13:26 p.m. - Spirit Box - "E_____".

What did the friends see while in this area of the battlefield? It has been retold for years that a "vortex" is on the hill that enables ghosts and spirits to move about freely to and from the area. What the friends saw was not a human, it was a black cat. As superstitious and peculiar as that may sound, it is interesting to note that during the Civil War at Fort McAllister in Savannah, Georgia, the men had a black cat mascot for the fort. War mascots were not uncommon and as sad as the tale is to repeat, the cat did die during a bombardment on the fort. The adorable critter was popular enough that his death was noted in an official report by the fort.

Perhaps the vortex at Little Round Top could enable spirits to travel in an even more unexpected way than only between our world and the next. Maybe time is elusive in these circumstances and the history and modern times are one.

Thursday April 1, 2010

EVP session taken while walking up the hill from Plum Run near Devils Den to the top of Little Round Top.

*By Plum Run.

7:55 p.m. - Digital Recorder - Whispering.

7:56 p.m. - Investigator - Hears an electrical sound.

7:57 p.m. - Two Investigators - Hear a noise.

7:59 p.m. - Investigator - Sees a blue light.

8:00 p.m. - Digital Recorder - Inaudible words.

8:01 p.m. - Investigator - Sees a face poking out from between two rocks near the top of Little Round Top.

*About half way up the hill, walking alongside the road.

8:02 p.m. - Investigator - Felt like someone was walking next to her.

8:02 p.m. - Investigator - Sees two flashes of light near the top of the hill.

8:03 p.m. - Investigator - Hears footsteps.

8:05 p.m. - Digital Recorder - "Get to the ground!" - male voice.

8:06 p.m. - Investigator - Hears footsteps.

8:07 p.m. - Investigator - Sees shadowy movement, as if someone is crouching down and looking around. There was some white mist around the figure.

8:07 p.m. - Investigator - Hears footsteps and has a pain in her neck.

8:08 p.m. - Investigator - Feels a pain in her abdomen, right lower quadrant.

8:08 p.m. - Investigator - Feels a cold spot.

8:08 p.m. - Investigator - "I have a pain in my right side".

8:08 p.m. - Digital Recorder - "I hurt you" - male voice.

8:08 p.m. - Digital Recorder - "Hello" - different voice than the "I hurt you" - male voice.

8:09 p.m. - Investigator - Sees shadowy feet marching.

8:10 p.m. - Digital Recorder - Disembodied gun shot.

8:10 p.m. - Investigator - "I see shadows and like something is down there"

8:10 p.m. - Digital Recorder - "Like me?" - male voice.

8:10 p.m. - Investigator - Sees a shadow.

8:13 p.m. - Digital Recorder - "Help me" - male voice.

8:17 p.m. - Investigator - "Are you part of Hood's Division?"

8:17 p.m. - Digital Recorder - "Help me" - male voice.

8:29 p.m. - Investigator - Is getting a headache. *

Just like other places in the park, the cries of "help me" still ring through time.

Headaches can be a physical sign that a strong paranormal or electromagnetic field is near the person.

The battlefield has been untouched by war for over a century, yet it seems that the men who fought and died on Little Round Top still hold strongly to their post at the end of the Union line, the flank, the anchor of the Northern army.

Triangular Field

October 16th, 2010

11:36:24 a.m. - Female investigator has her hair pulled.

11:36:50 a.m. - Investigators hear whispering, no EVPS on the digital recorder.

11:38:25 a.m. - Investigators hear footsteps, no EVPS on the digital recorder.

11:43:26 a.m. - Investigator sees movement out of the corner of her eye.

11:43:30 a.m. - Investigator - "What is your name?"

11:43:34 a.m. - Digital Recorder - Unreadable answer.

11:46:04 a.m. - Digital Recorder - Painful yell.

11:56:24 a.m. - Digital Recorder - "Come here!"

Just beyond Devil's Den, behind the rocky formation (if you view the front as the area where the parking lot is located), lies the Triangular Field. Best known as the area where technology is not welcomed: cameras fail, batteries are drained and other technical issues arise. Most avid Gettysburg ghost hunters will tell you that if you value your expensive equipment, do not take it into this field.

There are various reasons why these failures can happen, the common answer being that ghosts drain electrical equipment for food to help them manifest. This is not necessarily untrue, as areas that have high electromagnetic fields do come with a lot of paranormal and paranoid phenomenon, and being that the Triangular Field has no such sources the ghosts have to feed from somewhere to help them communicate with the living.

That may not be the only reason that they hate cameras and the like. Near the Triangular Field is Devils Den where the body of a soldier was moved from where he died and positioned for a photograph at the "sharp shooter" location in between the rocks.

Would it be naïve to think that this only happened once and that the dead did not take note of such unceremonious treatment of a dead comrade? Respectful treatment of the dead is part of society, and not doing such can cause rifts in the paranormal world and stir activity.

If this idea is true, then a few things can be learned about this location. Either this did happen to dead soldiers in that area, or they have not yet completely realized that they are separated from their fleshy tombs, or they are angry that this happened to a fellow soldier. Whichever is the answer, the lesson learned should be that whether one is a visitor, tourist, historian or paranormal investigator, always be respectful of the dead and the location in which they died.

Wheatfield

A whirlpool, that is how veterans of the battle at the Wheatfield described the scene with the fields once golden wheat trampled down and soaked with human blood. Within one day, the nineteen acres that encompasses the field changed hands six times.

Union troops under the command of Brigadier General Regis de Trobriand held the ground first with the men positioned smartly behind the stone wall at the end of the field. Charging through the woods on the other side of the field, where the marching can still be heard today, advance Brigadier General George Anderson's Georgia brigade.

Just like the scenario that played out for the men on Little Round Top, both Union and Confederate troops were running low on ammunition. To conserve ammunition, though it was a costly and dangerous maneuver, Anderson lined his men directly in front of the stone wall and ordered the men to go forward.

As the ammunition ran lower, the Union decided to retreat away from the stone wall, leaving it open for a Confederate siege. Suddenly, in an effort to retrieve their lost, precious ground, the Union turned around in a bayonet charging and reclaimed their stony holding just in time for reinforcements for both sides to arrive. Between the buildings of the Rose Farm emerged General Joseph B. Kershaw and his South Carolina brigade to aid in the attack.

Back and forth the fight went until the Union troops withdrew from the bloody field under continuing assaults by the Confederates. If not for the ammunition running low, the outcome could have been different but things happen the way we know and look back on thinking why?

"I rallied the remainder of my brigade and Semines's at Rose's, with the assistance of Colonel Sorrel of Longstreet's staff, and advanced with them to the support of Wofford, taking position at the stone wall overlooking the forest to the right of Rose's house, some two hundred yards in front...That night we occupied the ground over which we had fought, with my left at the Peach Orchard, on the hill, and gathered the dead and wounded—a long list of brave and efficient officers and men. Captain Cunningham's company of the 2d Regiment was reported to have gone into action with forty men, of whom but four remained unhurt to bury their fallen comrades. My losses exceeded 600 men killed and wounded,—about one-half the force engaged".

-Brig. General Joseph Kershaw, C.S.A.

Eye witness accounts are rarely unbiased and give only one side to an event and how the speaker sees the event. Two different people can see the same even and recount two different stories. Even dates and the numbers of the dead can be off. Documents can list an account of dead, wounding and missing, although is missing really an accurate description for those men who are missing in this world but were probably wandering through the next?

March 1st, 2010

2:12:53 p.m. - Digital Recorder - "There's a house" – male voice.

2:20:54 p.m. - Investigator - "Did you want to fight in the war?"

2:20:59 p.m. - Digital Recorder - "Yes" – male voice. October 16th, 2010

2:30:31 p.m. - Digital Recorder - Loud bang.

2:32:00 p.m. - Digital Recorder - Muffled whisper.

2:34:14 p.m. - Investigator - "Can I sit on this rock with you?"

2:34:36 p.m. - Digital Recorder - "Hello" - male voice.

2:35:50 p.m. - Investigator - "I heard, the last time we were here, somebody talking about a house and a barn on the other side of the trees. Were you going to the house?"

2:36:53 p.m. - Digital Recorder - "There was a house" - male voice.

2:38:56 p.m. - Investigator - "I would like to ask you again what your name is?"

2:40:53 p.m. - Digital Recorder - "Hello" - male voice.

The house that is spoken of is undoubtedly the Rose Farm house.

"In the garden of the Rose house in full view,...nearly one hundred rebels

were buried. All around the barn, even within the house yards, within a few feet of the doors, were in numbers, the scantily buried followers of the Confederate cause. Two hundred and seventy-five were buried behind the barn; a rebel colonel was buried within a yard of the kitchen door".

- John Howard Wert, (Gettysburg citizen and teacher).

On a random trip through Gettysburg in March of 2012, two of us stopped by the Wheatfield again. Taking with us only the spirit box to see if we could catch a real time conversation on the sacred ground. For the most part, the ghosts were quiet, however, one did give us his name, Captain Stewart. There is a number of regiments that he could have belonged to and I have yet to find which one. Perhaps he will be willing to speak to you too.

DAY 3

(July 3rd, 1863)

Pickett's Charge

Thick, heavy and unrelentingly hot for the men in their heavy cotton uniforms, the summer weather was a torturous fiend taunting with only the slightest warm breezes blowing past the trees. A mix matched canvas of grays, browns and the occasional spots of blue lined the front of the full, green trees. Indomitable spirits in tattered uniforms.

With the rat tat tat of the snare drums, the line began to march forward side by side as brotherly comrades. The starred blue 'x' of the Confederate banner leading the way. Cannon shells blasted overhead, the soldier's paying little heed to the artillery bombardment that started hours earlier. Fate and the Angel of Death marching in stride with the soldier's as the distance between the men and their finish line at the clump of trees on the Union line shrank. Rat tat tat!

Cannon shells blasted over head again, knocking holes in the formations as a few fell into their targets. Here and there a man would look back at his fallen comrades whose blood now stained his uniform. Ahead of them, the red, white and blue stars and stripes of the Federal Flag blew. Closer to their mark, the Union line across from them opened fire in a volley of poisonous lead.

"Forward!" the command rang out.

"Charge!" another command was shouted.

In the hopelessness of the moment, regiments and divisions began to turn back; retreating to their own side of the field, away from the firing enemy. While Pickett's generals: Lewis Armistead, Richard Garnett, and James Kemper continued to lead their Virginians to the line. In a round of musket and cannon fire, Garnett and Kemper fell, one wounded and one dead. Armistead climbed over the stone wall at the Union mark only to be shot as well.

Men lay dying on the field, knowing that their end was coming as their life blood flowed from their bodies. In the suffering heat, some wished for death to come and end their pain. Other's wished for the battle to end in victory and hence be saved.

Within an hour, General Pickett's Division was destroyed and the South was dealt a wound that would never heal.

Three divisions numbering roughly between 12,500 and 15,000 soldiers, depending on whose account you read, crossed the treacherous mile of open field. Within an hour, half of this number was dead, dying, wounded or captured.

March 14th, 2010

*Confederate side of the line

8:45:10 a.m. - Investigator hears a man's voice.

9:20:15 a.m. - Investigator - "What is your name?"

9:21:02 a.m. - Digital Recorder - " Anderson "

October 16th, 2010

* Union side of the line

6:12:24 p.m. Investigator - "Were you with Armistead?"

6:12:27 p.m. Digital Recorder - "Yes."

General Richard Garnett, against General Lee's orders, rode his horse during the charge. Courageously he drove his men forward until he was shot from his horse within sixty yards of the stone wall. His body was never identified. *May 15th, 2011*

*At the Union line

5:31:41 - Investigator - "Does anybody here know the whereabouts of General Garnett's body or what happened to him?"

5:32:04 p.m. - Digital Recorder - "I know."

The other divisions involved in the charge were commanded by Brigadier General J. Johnston Pettigrew and Major General Isaac R.

Trimble. The corps commanders were Lieutenant General James Longstreet with his First Corps and Lieutenant General A.P. Hill's Third Corps. Their ranks were made up of brave men from Virginia , North Carolina , Mississippi , Alabama , and Tennessee .

At 2pm the charge began, the goal being to reach and cross the Union line; the intended sight, a clump of trees at what is known as "The Angle". At the same time, a Confederate Calvary under the command of J.E.B. Stuart would circle around behind the Union line, thereby surrounding the Union at the center of the battlefield. The attack was a surprise to the Union Yankees, with the blazing summer heat; many thought they might have a day of reprieve from the fighting. Since both sides of their line had already been attacked, the middle of the line seemed the safest place at that moment.

The end of the battle came quickly; the wounded and surviving Confederates retreated back to their side of the field. Some began the retreat while the others were still marching forward. Those who did not make it back to the line either lay dead or dying on the fields of Gettysburg or were in the hands of the Union army. General Lee made the orders to retreat after the failed charge and on July 4th the Army of Northern Virginia made its way back across the Mason Dixon line into the South. If J.E.B. Stuart's Calvary would not have been cut off en route, the battle of Gettysburg could have had a different conclusion.

* To break the infantry down – Corps, Division, Brigade, Regiment. Several regiments make a brigade, several brigades make a division, several divisions make a corps.

October 16, 2010

*Union Line of Pickett's Charge

6:00:45 p.m. - EMF - EMF detector blinked middle of the EMF detector.

6:12:06 p.m. - Investigator - "What is your name?"

6:15:28 p.m. - Investigator - "Anything else?"

6:15:30 p.m. - Digital Recorder - "Yes" - male voice.

6:18:44 p.m. - Digital Recorder "Hey, get back here!" - male voice.

6:18:56 p.m. - Digital Recorder "Hey!" - male voice.

6:18:58 p.m. - Equipment - Equipment Malfunction - digital recorder screen went blank and flashed the 'one sec' and then went back to normal.

6:19:46 p.m. - Digital Recorder - "Help!" - male voice.

Date: May 15th, 2011

*At the Angle- Union side of the charge.

5:33:07 p.m. - Digital Recorder - "Hey" – male voice.

5:34:26 p.m. - Digital Recorder - "Mommy" – young male voice.

*Walking towards the old cyclorama.

5:35:54 p.m. - Digital Recorder - "Come here" – male voice.

5:37:45 p.m. - Digital Recorder - Deep exhaling breath.

5:39:05 p.m. - Digital Recorder - "Help me" – male voice.

5:39:35 p.m. - Digital Recorder - "(Hear or help) me" – male voice.

*Walking away from the cyclorama.

5:39:42 p.m. - Digital Recorder - "Hey, it's (me or Meade)" – male voice.

"Well, it is all over now. The battle is lost, and many of us are prisoners, many are dead, many wounded, bleeding and dying. Your Soldier lives and mourns and but for you, my darling, he would rather, a million times *rather, be back there with his dead, to sleep for all time in an unknown grave."*

- Major General George Pickett, CSA, to his fiancée, July 4, 1863

In view of the Union line at Pickett's Charge

Gettysburg Cemetery

"Oh, you dead, who at Gettysburg have baptized with your blood the second birth of Freedom in America, how you are to be envied! I rise from a grave whose wet clay I have passionately kissed, and I look up and see Christ spanning this battle-field with his feet and reaching fraternally and lovingly up to heaven."

-William Samuel

(New York Times, July 6th, 1863)

Through the rows of dead, both marked and unmarked graves loom. Testaments as to how important remembering the dead and the Afterlife is to many.

Usually, I am not one for investigating cemeteries so that the dead may rest in peace, yet not all of those who are dead and buried in a cemetery are at peace. All the men for names are unknown have been buried and to be forgotten by time. As I walk through the sacred ground I tell the men, "If you tell me what your name is, I will try and help you be remembered".

At least one ghosts answered my call, for a man named Horace came forward to share his name. I could not hear anything else. So for the paranormal enthusiasts or investigating who wants to help the dead be remembered, they are there waiting for your help.

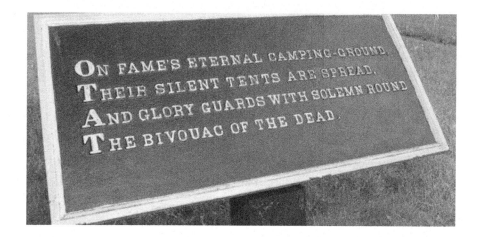

Directions: Baltimore Pike, Gettysburg

The Ghost on the White Horse

One ghostly encounter on the battlefield occurred in the heat of battle on the second day of that fateful July. By this point in time, thousands of men on both sides already laid dead in the golden fields of Gettysburg . However, this particular ghost was not one of these recently deceased soldiers. In actuality he had died sixty four years prior to Gettysburg and several states away.

The account of the event was told by Union General Oliver Hunt. Hunt's men had the great task of defending Little Round Top from the onslaught of Confederate troops charging up the hill. Just like Chamberlain and the infamous 20th Maine , Hunt's men were also out of ammunition. The general was prepared to order a retreat when a figure dressed in the clothing of a Revolutionary War soldier on a white horse appeared in front of his men. With a wave of his hand, the ghost sent the men charging down the hill in a surprise greeting to their opponents.

The story became so popular that the Secretary of State, Edward Stanton, ordered an investigation into the incident.

I would not besmirch the General's character to say that the story could have been an exaggeration to say that the Union has a Founding Father's blessing. It is possible that the General did see a Revolutionary soldier awoken from his slumber by the sounds and smells of battle. During the Revolution, Pennsylvania was the site of battles and winter encampments, namely Valley Forge and the Battle of the Brandywine .

With my own eyes, I had the surprising opportunity to witness the apparition of a man dressed in the clothing of a Revolutionary War soldier during an investigation near Pine Grove Furnace, twenty some miles from the town of Gettysburg. I cannot say if he was on a mission or was a runaway because he was oblivious to my presence as he made his hurried stride through the woods. Dressed in a long blue coat much like one can see in paintings of French soldiers in the Revolution. The question is, was the man really our first President General George Washington.

Although with the great succession at rest, President Washington should have no reason to return to Gettysburg . Yet, reports still persist that a man in a tri-corn hat riding a white horse encased in a luminous glow has been seen riding across the battlefield and then disappearing without a glance or word to those watching his supernatural visit.

If the story is true it would certainly give a few people a new way to view how the deceased travel after their deaths.

Gettysburg offers quite an opportunity for paranormal investigators. Despite the many tragic deaths, Gettysburg is one of the few places in this book that I have been to that I never felt afraid or paranoid at day or night to be in the park. The unknown can be scary and there are ghosts and inhuman entities out there that are made up of dark energy and can be unpredictable, I have seen and experienced this for myself.

This is why Gettysburg is such a truly spectacular place because it is active and for the most part it is not dark. It can be sad, depressing and emotionally twisting but the hosts that reside there are do not remain with the sole intention of harming the living. Perhaps it is because of sadness in the place that the negative does not lurk. Sometimes, the strongest emotion can diminish the bad.

IRON FURNACES
PENNSYLVANIA AND VIRGINIA

It was during an investigation for my previous book, *Ghosts and Haunted Places of Pennsylvania*, that I pondered the theory, *'could a ghost haunt the place where the mechanism of their death was manufactured'*. I received an answer to this question at Codorus Iron Furnace in York County, Pennsylvania. This particular furnace was used to manufacture cannon balls during the American Revolution.

November 20th, 2010

2:20:55 p.m. - Investigator - "Are there any soldiers here that were killed by cannon balls manufactured here?"

2:21:29 p.m. - Digital Recorder - "Yes" – male voice.

This theory has been brought up by others in regards to places such as: the Remington Arms Factory and the Winchester Mystery House. The house was built by Sarah Winchester, widow of William Wirt Winchester, and heiress to the Winchester fortune. She believed that she was being haunted by the spirits of those who were murdered by Winchester rifles and built the mystery mansion in order to either appease or hide from them.

Codorus Iron Furnace

While factories produced rifles, iron furnaces produced cannon balls. Although these furnaces may seem a part of a far distant past, a few were still operational during the Civil War.

Caledonia Iron Furnace, Pennsylvania

Caledonia Iron Furnace

Dusk was closing in on a rainy, cloudy April day, as we drove down Pine Grove road to this historic little furnace stack. Thousands of trees lined either side of the road, planted during the Great Depression by the Civilian Conservation Corps to replace the acres cut down for use at the local furnaces. Compared to the well-preserved Pine Grove Iron Furnace located thirteen miles further down the same road, Caledonia Furnace seems to be little more than a rock pile back dropped by a vast forest.

Originally built in 1837 in the rural area near the Village of Caledonia located on the Conecocheaque Creek. (Locations for iron furnaces were chosen based primarily on the close proximity of natural resources. This is why so many furnaces are located in the countryside, near forests and water). Caledonia Furnace, has been known as Caledonia Works, Caledonia Forge and Steven's Furnace, named for it's owner politician Thaddeus Stevens.

In June of 1863, during the American Civil War and a month before the battle at Gettysburg , a Confederate Calvary under the leadership of General Jubal Early burnt the furnace and its surrounding buildings to the ground. This event was an isolated incident by the Confederates in retaliation to Thaddeus Stevens' hate of the South and their way of life.

"I fear we shall forget justice to living rebels and to slaughtered dead, and shall overlook our future safety, and deal too mercifully with assassins and traitors...to permit the ringleaders to escape with impunity is absolute cruelty...take their property, if you allow them to live...Take the riches of those nobles who would found an empire on slavery."

- an excerpt from a speech given by Thaddeus Stevens at Appomattox on April 10, 1865; one day after General Robert E. Lee's surrender to Ulysses S. Grant. In these words, it can be clearly seen his distaste for the Southern Confederacy that he had been outspoken about since the start of the Civil War in 1861.

Two years after the burning of Caledonia furnace, the Civil War officially ended. Stevens no longer needed to fear another Confederate attack on his property; yet, from that time until his death on August 11, 1868, Stevens made no effort to rebuild his iron works. The reason assumed to be that the furnace did not generate a good source of income. The land remained untouched until the 1920s when the Pennsylvania Alpine Club reconstructed the furnace and the blacksmith shop. The reconstructed stack is only about half the size, possibly less, of the original furnace and it's questionable if it stands in the same location as the original.

With historical facts backing that male workers and soldiers would have been at the furnace, it is quite remarkable that the EVP that was caught was of a female spirit.

April 19th, 2011 at 5:48 p.m.

Investigator "What is your name?"

"It's Jennifer". Her answer was loud but soft, clear and without an accent.

There is little information on the furnace, let alone who all would have lived there. The owner, Thaddeus Stevens, was not married, had no children and did not live in the area. This concludes that the ghost has no ties to him. The wife of a worker, perhaps, or someone linked to another era before or after the furnace was built and in operation? For now, Jennifer remains our mysterious ghost. Which lead to more questions with no answers....so far.

"I should fear to be haunted by the ghosts of murdered patriots stalking forth from their premature grave in their blood shrouds."

- Thaddeus Stevens (Appomattox, April 10, 1865).

Directions: Caledonia Furnace is located at the intersection of Route 30 and Pine Grove Furnace Road near Chambersburg and Gettysburg.

Hopewell Iron Furnace, Pennsylvania

Over a hundred miles east of the Caledonia furnace sits Hopewell Furnace. Ironmaster Mark Bird, from whom the town of Birdsboro was named, founded the furnace site in 1771, it closed in 1883 and still remains one of the most well-preserved sites in the state of Pennsylvania, and has fourteen restored structures. Surrounding the historical site on 848 acres, which is mostly trees, and French Creek State Park.

This particular furnace did not see any battles; instead it was favored with an economic boom because of the war producing pig iron for the Union army. A few of the men who worked at the furnace were quick to enlist. Henry Miner was one of the first volunteers to go, enlisting in Captain James McKnight's Ringgold Light Artillery. At least a dozen men followed Miner's choice.

After the battle of Gettysburg in 1863, two more men, Adam Bard and Samuel Williams also left Hopewell to join the 42nd Pennsylvania Emergency Militia Regiment. Six of the men who left the furnace to fight died during the war: Henry Hauck, Fred Mosteller, Henry Care, Daniel Buckley, Henry Nanback and Daniel Hunsberger.

How many of the former workers or other ghostly soldiers haunt the site is unclear, most stories center around a woman in a long dress that walks around the site and tales of the "Gray Devil". The name Gray Devil may sound like one of those even harder to believe, tall tale ghost stories. However, the story is not as hard to believe as it seems, there was a cold-blooded man behind the name, a criminal whose true identity was never known. They say he traveled from Canada to the Carolinas and back, making his way through towns, stealing and committing other heinous acts.

In Lancaster County, a warrant was finally issued for the mysterious mans arrest. When he was caught in upstate New York, a deputy sheriff from Lancaster went to bring him back to Pennsylvania for trial. On the way, the two stopped at the Blue Ball Tavern, where the criminal made his escape and eventually ended up in Berks County, near the area of the furnace. It was here that he finally met his end, by falling in love with a raven-haired beauty, who upon finding out his true identity was enraged enough to lend a hand in his capture. She set up a meeting time for him and stood by as he was arrested by the authorities from Lancaster, Berks and Chester counties. In the ensuring struggle, he was shot in the shoulder, falling to the ground.

The devil died alone in a cell in Lancaster County jail, finding a new freedom in death. At night, the man without a name rides a silver steed down old Hopewell Road. Searching for his next victim.

Directions:2 Mark Bird Lane, Elverson

Catherine Iron Furnace, Virginia

This furnace located in Chancellorsville was transformed from a household goods furnace in the early 1800s was reopened to produce forge munitions for the Confederate army. Like most places that were beneficial to one of the armies, it fell to destruction by the opposing Union army. At least part of the furnace still exists.

During the war, this furnace had little trouble finding men to work at it, as those who did not want to fight in the war would practically hire themselves out for nothing as long as it kept them from the guns and sabers of battle.

It is a gorgeous, historical site surrounded by young trees. While I must admit that there are no ghostly recordings in the area, chances are one could find a few residual ones if someone would dare to try. Iron furnaces were always run near water and among the ores and stones used in the production of goods were: limestone and quartz. Water, quartz and limestone have all been connected to a residual haunting. There are knowledgeable people in the world who will dispute the accuracy of this, saying that: even though limestone, quartz and water can conduct electricity does not mean that they create the right field for paranormal activity. They may be right, but there are also people in the know who will disagree. Whichever side is correct, I have yet to visit an iron furnace that did not have either residual or intelligent haunting or both.

Directions: George Washington and Jefferson National Forest, off of Katherine Furnace Road, off of Rt 685

MANASSAS
VIRGINIA

During the first battle of Manassas, a true battle was fought, unlike any before it. It was the first time that the Union heard the "Rebel Yell", it was the first time that many young men learned what war meant, and for many it was the first time they had witnessed other men die before their very eyes. As the first battle came to a close, the Union soldiers retreated; running head on into a cluster of fleeing carriages, turning a partially organized retreat into a frantic escape.

It was quite an embarrassing moment for the North, senators and citizens had brought their families to watch the battle. They believed that it would be a quick and entertaining end to the uprising South. For the first time, the Union in the North realized that the South would fight to the death for what they believed in. Which, despite what many of us have learned in history books, most of the South was not fighting for the right to keep slaves; no, there was more to it than that: there was the freedom to secede, the rights of the states and the rights to not be heavily taxed by the North. The South wanted to live their lives in their own way.

There were two battles of Manassas, the 1st and 2nd. In the North, they called it the battle of Bull Run, after the nearby creek; in the South it was named after the town.

The Judith Henry House

Judith Henry was an old woman by the time the war came to her doorstep, she was in her 80s, bedridden and unwilling to leave her home. She lived in the house with her daughter, Ellen, and a servant girl named Lucy. Hugh, one of her sons would check in on the family periodically and he was there during the battle. With the help of soldiers, the family considered moving to a neighbor's house a mile away, then changed their minds to hide in the spring house. When the spring house became just as unsafe as the farm house, Judith Henry, begged to be put back into her own bed.

Union and Confederate soldiers both fought in the front hallway of the house. Eventually the Confederates took it over, using it as a sharpshooter's post. The Union fired cannon balls at the house in order to chase out the Rebel soldiers, one of the shells burst through the walls of Mrs. Henry's bedroom, shattering her bed and knocking her to the floor and causing injuries to her head, neck and causing the loss of part of one of her feet. She died later that day from her injuries. Along with Mrs. Henry, 5,000 soldiers also perished, many dying in the fields around her house during the climax of the battle.

Investigation September 3rd, 2011 in the field behind the Henry House
2:45 p.m. – EVP – "What are you doing here?"

Most of the attention given to civilian casualties during the war centers on Jenny Wade, the only citizen killed during the battle of Gettysburg. Henry, on the other hand, was the first civilian killed at the start of the war; an unexpected causality at the beginning of the war. Her house was in ruins by the time the battle was over, the only pieces left were fragments of wood and the chimney stack. The Judith Henry house that sits on Manassas battlefield is a reconstruction of what once was her home.

The Black Moon Paranormal Society conducted an investigation inside the reconstructed home on September 3rd, 2011. After the investigation, the crew gathered together to discuss the evidence to find that not one of them had a personal experience. A review of the digital recorders afterwards, they heard a woman say, *"Oh, my God!"*

Locals who live near the battlefield have reported sightings of a woman dressed in an older style dress walking the roads near where the battlefield took place. She always disappears before anyone has a chance to question her about whom she is and why she walks the roads at night. This apparition is not necessarily Judith Henry, although the consequences of the battle on that day of July 21, 1861may have left a mark on her spirit. Trapping a younger version of the woman's spirit in a time loop of her home land or it could be a different spirit entirely, one that originated around the same time period, whose life and circumstances of her death are a mystery.

The apparition could also be Judith's daughter, Ellen. She did not die during the battle, but the scenes and emotional turmoil that befell her that day could have caused her spirit to remain. She had a dead Union soldier fall at her feet in the front hallway of the house, she lost her mother and she lost her hearing because of the battle. During the cannon bombardment, Ellen hid in the big chimney; in pictures from months after the battle, the chimney was one of the only parts of the house still standing. The bombardment caused such injury to her ears from a violent concussion. If the trauma of that day did not cause Ellen to stick around, there were other families in the area who also felt the war too close to home.

The Stone House

During the First Battle: Despite the chaos and destruction

encompassing the fields and woods around it, the Stone House stood unflinching as men were carried through its doors. The traffic through the house was heavier from the battle than during its early years as a stop on the Fauquier and Alexandria Turnpikes. It's location along the roads, as well as a sturdy foundation made it an ideal location for a field hospital. Flags had to be flown in the windows of the house to mark it as a hospital, in the hopes that the barrage of gunfire on the house would calm, but it barely did so. As soon as the fighting shifted away from the house, more men piled into the walls.

Investigation September 3rd, 2011 at 3:05p.m by the front door.
3:07:50 p.m. - EVP – "Get help...get the door!"
3:08:17 p.m. - EVP – "Help!"
3:11:36 p.m. - EVP – "Carry him in!"

Numerous reports about the hospital spoke of the mounting filth and dirt that piled within the house, creating a smell so disdainful that no visitors remained for long. At one point it was documented that nearly 100 arms lay in piles on the floor. "In this building were 32 wounded, many of them dreadfully mangled by cannon shot. There was but a single surgeon, and he was young and apparently inefficient. Men lay on the floor with their clotted wounds still undressed. Some had died and not been removed..." – remarked one unknown source. That single surgeon was Dr. James Harris of the 1st Rhode Island Infantry, who remained after the rest of his regiment retreated after the battle.

At that time, the house came under Confederate control and thirty-six wounded Union men were sent to Confederate prisons. At least one officer died in the house, Colonel John S. Slocum of the 2nd Rhode Island Infantry. During the Second Battle: Most of the events remained the same as the second battle of Bull Run drove through the town. At the end of the battle, the Confederates again had control of the house; only this time, instead of arresting the wounded soldiers inside, they were paroled. The Matthews family who owned the house, and who had left during the battles, sold it in 1865.

As investigators perused the property in September of 2011, the faint echo of drum beats were heard beside the house on the right side of the front door. Inside the home, one of the investigators heard whisper and boots walking, while one of the female investigators was touched on her back. Even though the last ambulance rolled away from the property on September 2nd, 1862, there were at least a few soldiers who were left behind.

The Stone Bridge

"When I was on the first half of the bridge, I felt this wave of sadness. It passed when we were near the creek bed". - Adam Clauser, Paranormal Investigator.

During the First Battle:
    Down the road from the Stone and Henry Houses is the Stone Bridge. During the first battle of Bull Run, the bridge was more of a crossing point for the Union Army, both Brigadier General Daniel Tyler and Brigadier General Robert C. Schenck had men on the bridge at one point. Confederates under Colonel Nathan "Shanks" Evans responded to the bridge to intercept Tyler's men. Little more than a skirmish came out of it. Quickly the soldiers moved towards the nearby hills where a high number of other soldiers were converging. During the Second

Battle: During the second battle, the Union used the bridge for a path of retreat, with the men in the rear destroying it.

Investigation September 3rd, 2011 at 3:05p.m
3:40:10 p.m. - Investigator – "Were you here for the first or second battle?"
3:40:17 p.m. - EVP – "Second"
3:44:19 p.m. – "Turn around quick!"

The Stone Bridge after the 2nd battle of Manassas

The Unfinished Railroad

One of the most important landmarks at Manassas is the "Unfinished Railroad". This stretch of a man made earthwork aided to the Confederate victory during the second battle and without it, the Confederacy would probably have lost the battle.

During their retreat after the first battle, Union soldiers took notice to the deep bed where a railroad should have been; it was partially overgrown and hidden within the trees. Unfortunately for them, before the second battle began, General "Stonewall" Jackson already had his men in position there. The fighting was heavy, intense and centered on that area. While Jackson's men held the Union at bay, it gave General Lee a chance to use a few tactics of his own. Strategy, not numbers, was the key to this Confederate victory and, demonstrated why Jackson was Lee's right hand man.

There was six of is altogether when we investigated the railroad bed; a large group for a large area and, with the ability to spread out over the area. It was a chilly September day, heavy clouds traveled over head and a threat of rain persisted throughout the afternoon. The area was clear of people around us, save for a lone jogger.
The time period of our visit was just a matter of days after the anniversary of the second battle of Bull Run happened, a month and a half after the anniversary of the 149th anniversary of the first battle. The paranormal energy would have been on a down slope off of the peak time that correlated with the death dates of many men.

One of the team members stepped off the bed path, moving slightly into the woods where he captured an EVP with a desperate sounding plea of, "get away". In a different direction, another team member was snapping pictures of the landscape.

In the distance, in the photos is a man dressed in Union blue. A man that was not there when the picture was taken, and not one of the six saw him come or go.

This is a close up of the same shot.

Catching anything paranormal related is a rarity, 90% of the time what you are looking at is not real. However, if you believe what the investigators say, that not a single one of them saw this man while they were investigating. Then perhaps you are catching a glimpse into the rare and remarkable.

Directions: 6511 Sudley Road, Manassas, VA 20109

SHENANDOAH VALLEY
VIRGINIA

Rain poured down, darkening the night. Through the mist and fog, a team of horses thundered forward, snorting, straining to pull the stage coach strapped to them, galloping as if the hounds of Hell were chasing them. Their new master cracked the whip, shouting at the team to go faster. His words were lost to the wind.

In the distance, behind them two shadowed figures lurched forward; the two lone riders gained speed on the weighted down coach. The driver cracked the whip again, his urgency to reach the Federal pickets mounting. Drops of hail clanged off the top of the stage coach, causing the man to pull his mud splattered jacket tighter around his chest.

He turned, looking at the riders following him, sweat dripping off his brow despite the chill of the rain. Turning his eyes back to the road, it was a straight trail leading to where Union General Nathaniel P. Banks waited in Winchester. Unaware that General "Stonewall" Jackson and his army were marching toward the Union army.

From the corner of the driver's eyes, he saw the clear vision of a Confederate soldier beside the coach, aiming his weapon. The driver also drew his pistol, placing his finger on the trigger. A loud explosion rang out, and the coach driver fell over dead. His wild, racing team of horses urged to a stop. It was not a Confederate bullet that killed the man, lighting had struck him. Killing him instantly.

On the anniversary of May 24, 1862, a ghostly white team of horses is seen pulling the stage coach driven by the charred remains of a spy trying to deliver a message that will never arrive. The road that the man traveled is said to be the Valley Pike near Winchester, a two-lane road that opened in 1840. There are no widely known historical accounts of this incident, and no record of a spy being struck by lightning. On the date in question, Jackson's Shenandoah Campaign was nearing an end and the army had moved on to Winchester, Virginia.

Directions: U.S. Highway 11, previously the Valley Pike

While the stage coach driver was meeting with fate, another spy was having better luck with their espionage. Belle Boyd was more than lucky, during the war she was caught spying once, if she had been a man, she more than likely would have been executed on the spot. Instead she was released with the threat of death. Before she was even a spy, she murdered a Union soldier on July 4th, 1861 for taking down the Confederate flag flying outside her family's hotel and for cursing at her mother. She was exonerated of that crime as well, the crime that ignited a spark inside her to act upon her Confederate sympathies.

During the early years of the war she managed to charm a Union officer by the name of Captain Daniel Kelly. From Kelly she collected information on the Union army that was delivered to Confederate officers by her slave, Eliza Hopewell. Then in 1862, while Union General James Shields and his staff gathered in the parlor of her family's hotel she hid in a closet to eavesdrop on the men.

That night, following the secret meeting, Belle herself rode through Union lines, using false papers and bluffing her way to Confederate scout Colonel Turner Ashby. On May 23, 1862 she ran to greet General "Stonewall" Jackson and his men, urging an officer to pass on that the Union force was small. The cost of passing on the information was a few bullet holes in her skirt; the reward was a personal thank you from the general, an honorary aide-de-camp and captain positions and the Southern Cross of Honor.

In the light of the moon, I saw a woman running down the road, she looked as if she was in a great hurry. Her long dress reminded me of another time: a blue dress with a white apron and bonnet. She turned, taking a path into the woods where in the distance I could see the light of a camp fire.

Boyd was arrested two more times on July 29th, 1862 and December 1, 1863. After her December arrest, sick with typhoid she was released and sent to Europe. During her life, she married three times and became a stage actress. She died in 1900 in the United States.

The cottage in which Belle lived in while Union officers occupied her families hotel is also haunted by Belle and a man with an unknown name. It was in this cottage that she hatched her plans to warn General "Stonewall" Jackson during the battle of Fort Royal.

Witnesses have reported footsteps, voices, lights turning off, a woman humming and a piano playing.

Directions: 101 Chester St. New Market, Virginia

POINT LOOKOUT
MARYLAND

Lighthouses are symbols of safety and hope; a guiding light in the darkness. The exclusion is the Point Lookout lighthouse, a guiding light to darkness and despair. Below the glowing light of the tower stood an army garrison called Fort Lincoln, a port, a short-term city, a hospital and from 1863-1865, a demoralizing prisoner of war camp.

While not as inhumane and deadly as Andersonville, Point Lookout was still a frightening place to be imprisoned. It is considered one of the worst Union run prison camps of the war. Roughly 50,000 soldiers came to the prison, 4,000 of those men never left alive. A small percentage to be sure, but it was not the wounds of battle that caused these men to go to an untimely death. Disease, starvation and violence were instead the culprits.

"I have heard men pray to be made sick that the appetite might be taken away. The prisoners being so poorly clad, and the Point so much exposed to cold, it caused them great suffering. Every intensity cold night from four to seven prisoners would freeze to death".

- Rev. J. B. Traywick

The prison was designed to hold 10,000 men at a time. What ended up happening, just the same with other prison camps, the number swelled beyond capacity. Between 12,000 and 20,000 prisoners were there at one time, which meant sixteen men to a tent, causing dangerously unsanitary conditions.

Of the soldiers who would rotate through guarding the prisoners, members of the U.S.C.T. Regiments (United States Colored Troops). The African American soldiers who fought in the war were just as brave and honorable as all the other men who fought in the war. Unfortunately, even honorable men have their limits and when the U.S.C.T. Regiments found themselves guarding the Confederate soldiers, a few of them also found their old slave masters. To point out, not all slave handlers mistreated their slaves, some were quite kind. Those past slave owners had little to fear from their guards and there were several acts of unregrettable kindness between the two. Life, as we know, is not always made up of kindness, and some of the owners did brutally mistreat the African Americans. It was those men who found themselves realizing that the mistakes of their past were coming back to haunt them.

One apparition in particular stands out above any other, one of a man running as fast as his long legs will carry him away from the Hell of prison life. He is seen during the day running from where the old smallpox hospital was located on grounds towards the woods. A Confederate soldier trying to escape after being allowed hospital duty. If he did escape, it seems as though he never made it away from Point Lookout.

*To note: half of the POW stockade has been washed away by erosion and the Chesapeake Bay , but the location is still there as well as a cemetery and memorial.

POW Memorial to the Confederate Soldiers at Point Lookout

Glossary of Paranormal Investigation Related Terms

EVPs – (Electronic Voice Phenomenon) – are voices that are "captured" using a digital recorder or spirit box that have no living source. There are various theories as to how it works and the potential of it; the simple answer is that ghosts and spirits often speak on different wave lengths than those of us who are living. If you are using a digital recorder and hear an extra voice in the play back that was not there before, you may have yourself a ghost and an EVP. Investigators Tip: When listening to a digital recorder, pay attention to any static or electrical noises that happen on the recorder, ghosts frequently talk within this static called "white noise". They may not always use the white noise, and at times can be heard without it, but for new investigators, it is something to listen for.

EMF – (Electromagnetic Force) – when a magnetic field induces an electrical current; this is said to be, at times, caused by ghosts.

Spirit Box – is a device that is used by paranormal investigators that is able to give real time responses. Unlike a digital recorder that a person has to go back and listen to afterwards, this device is, essentially, a modified radio that quickly sweeps through radio stations and produces a high frequency white noise. This little box has proved very useful during investigations.

Author's Note

Dear Reader, thank you for reading Ghosts and Haunted Places of the *American Civil War.* This time period in history has held a special interest to me for over a decade. I hope that through the knowledge that this book offers, some of those who died will know that they are not forgotten and find some peace.

The 1860s were a tormented time in our history, having family on both sides of the war and living near Gettysburg, PA has introduced me to a level of emotion and respect that one would not think possible of a past that has never touched us.

It is my hope that through writing these books, more of the deceased can find peace and know that they are not forgotten. Perhaps one of their stories will touch you as well and make you want to find out more in order to help them.

In the end, may we all be able to move on with a peaceful mind.

If you wish to contact the author or have your story featured in an upcoming book, please e-mail:

blackmoonparanormalsociety@yahoo.com.

In Memory Of

To My Ancestors Who Served: Hiriam McCoy and the Gilreath Brother's from North Carolina who fought in the war.

And to:

A Confederate soul who has touched me deeply.

Richard B. Garnett

(November 21, 1817 - July 3, 1863)

And all the men and women whose bodies and hearts perished in the American Civil War.

References

All investigation information has been collected by the Black Moon Paranormal Society.

Black Moon Paranormal Society. Archives and Investigations. www.blackmoonparanormalsociety.com. (2009-2012).

Some of the historical information has been gathered directly from the signs, plaques and information centers at the historic places and battles. The places visited first hand are: Antietam, Fredericksburg, Gettysburg, Manassas, Chowan University and some of the Iron Furnaces.

Historical Credits are also due to my wonderful history teachers in high school and college, who taught in a way that I would never forget the history.

Personal Accounts in this book are courtesy: members of the Black Moon Paranormal Society and anonymous people who have contacted me. Any correlation between the personal accounts and accounts recorded by others is strictly paranormal.

The 20th Maine & 15th Alabama at Little Round Top", http://www.brotherswar.com/Gettysburg-2e.htm (2 April 2011).

ABC Channel 6 Action News. *"Historic Discovery Made at Fort Mifflin"* http://www.11thpa.org/mifflin_find.html. (28 August 2006). (20 May 2011).

The American Civil War, *"The Battle of Gettysburg ".* – Thursday July 2, 1863

Belle Boyd. Civil War Stories, Ghost Stories. http://themoonlitroad.com/belle-boyd/ (April 4th, 2005) (July 24, 2012).

Boyer Jones, Shannon. *Ghosts and Haunted Places of Pennsylvania .* (2010).

Brann, James R. *"Defense of Little Round Top"*, America 's Civil War, (November, 1999). (8 June 2011).

Carnton Plantation and Battlefield. http://www.carnton.org/carnton_history.htm (2011) (10/15/2012).

"The Carter House: Haunted Tennessee". Ghosts of the Prairie. (2001) (7/24/2012).

Civil War Reference, "Kershaw's Brigade at Gettysburg ", http://www.civilwarreference.com/articles/detail.php?aricle=120. (2011). (2 April 2011).

Coco, Gregory A. "Confederates Killed in Action at Gettysburg ". (Gettysburg , PA : Thomas Publications, 2001). 63, 99.

Coleman, Dorcas. *"Who's Afraid of Ghosts?"* http://dnr.maryland.gov/naturalresources/fall2001/ghosts.html. (10/17/2012).

Cunningham, Horace H. *Field Medical Services at the Battle of Manassas (Bull Run)*. (Athens , Georgia . University of Georgia Press , 1968).

Fort Mifflin : The Fort That Saved America . " Fort Mifflin ". http://fortmifflin.us//about.html. (15 May 2011).

Highsmith, Carol M. and Landphair, Ted. Civil War Battlefields and Landmarks: A Photographic Tour. (Crescent Books, NY. 2003).

Howe Family Genealogy Forum. "William H. Howe of Mont. Co. PA, executed Fort Mifflin 1864; info and descendants". http://genforum.genealogy.com/howe/messages/4597.html (10 **March 2008**). (20 May 2011).

Shiloh National Military Park. National Park Service. www.nps.gov/shil/ (10/10/12).

"Some Events Connected with the Life of Judith Carter Henry". The Files of Manassas National Battlefield Park . http://www.nps.gov/mana/forteachers/upload/Res10_DeathofJudithHenry.pdf (10/17/12).

"The Spectral Stage of the Shenandoah Valley ". Blue & Gray: For Those Who Still Hear the Guns.(Blue & Gray Magazine, October, 1997). 47.

The Story of Tod Carter and the Civil War Battle of Franklin. http://m.youtube.com/#/watch?v=zRvy30D6ngA&desktop_uri=%2Fwatch%3Fv%3DzRvy30D6ngA **(Feb 16, 2010) (Oct 10, 2012).**

Sword, Wiley. *"The Other Stonewall"*. Civil War Times Illustrated. (February 1998, Vol: XXXVI Number 7). 36.

Taylor, Troy. "Belle Boyd/Confederate Spy". http://themoonlitroad.com/belle-boyd-confederate-spy/ (8/20/12).

Visit-Gettysburg.com, "Devils Den in Gettysburg ", http://www.visit-gettysburg.com/devils-den-in-gettysburg.html (2 April 2011).

Wagner, Stephen. *"Ghost Encounters at Gettysburg"*. About.com. http://paranormal.about.com/od/hauntedplaces/a/gettysburg-ghosts_3.htm

Coming Soon:

Ghosts and Haunted Places of the East Coast: Coastal Towns, Lighthouses and Shipwrecks.

Summer of 2013

And

Ghosts and Haunted Places of Pennsylvania 2

December of 2013

ABOUT THE AUTHOR

Shannon Boyer Jones was born and raised in Central Pennsylvania and later North Carolina. She attended Chowan College where she achieved a Bachelor of Science degree in Criminal Justice, with minors a minor in History. She has travelled throughout the East Coast of the United States, Europe and Australia.
Spurred on by an interest in the paranormal that she found in her youth. she founded the Black Moon Paranormal Society in 2009.

Photograph is by Laura Fealtman, photography.